THE
HUNGERING
DARK

THE
HUNGERING
DARK

Frederick Buechner

THE SEABURY PRESS • NEW YORK

Second Paperback Printing
1981
The Seabury Press
815 Second Avenue
New York, N.Y. 10017

Printed in the United States of America.

Library of Congress Catalog Card Number: 68-29987
ISBN: 0-8164-2314-8

To
My Former Students and Colleagues
at the Phillips Exeter Academy

Contents

part I

THE SEARCH

Thou hast said, "Seek ye my face."
My heart says to thee,
"Thy face, Lord, do I seek."
Hide not thy face from me.

PSALM 27:8–9

1

The Face in the Sky

And in that region there were shepherds out in the field, keeping watch over their flock by night. And an angel of the Lord appeared to them, and the glory of the Lord shone around them, and they were filled with fear. And the angel said to them, "Be not afraid; for behold, I bring you good news of a great joy, which will come to all the people; for to you is born this day in the city of David a Savior, who is Christ the Lord. And this will be a sign for you: you will find a babe wrapped in swaddling clothes and lying in a manger.   LUKE 2:8–12

As the Italian film *La Dolce Vita* opens, a helicopter is flying slowly through the sky not very high above the ground. Hanging down from the helicopter in a kind of halter is the life-size statue of a man dressed in robes with his arms outstretched so that he looks almost as if he is flying by himself, especially when every once in a while the camera cuts out the helicopter and all you can see is the statue itself with the rope around it. It flies over a field where some men are working in tractors and causes a good deal of excitement. They wave their hats and hop around and yell, and then one of them recognizes who it is a statue of and shouts in Italian,

"Hey, it's Jesus!" whereupon some of them start running along under the plane, waving and calling to it. But the helicopter keeps on going, and after a while it reaches the outskirts of Rome, where it passes over a building on the roof of which there is a swimming pool surrounded by a number of girls in bikinis basking in the sun. Of course they look up too and start waving, and this time the helicopter does a double take as the young men flying it get a good look at the girls and come circling back again to hover over the pool where, above the roar of the engine, they try to get the girls' telephone numbers, explaining that they are taking the statue to the Vatican and will be only too happy to return as soon as their mission is accomplished.

During all of this the reaction of the audience in the little college town where I saw the film was of course to laugh at the incongruity of the whole thing. There was the sacred statue dangling from the sky, on the one hand, and the profane young Italians and the bosomy young bathing beauties, on the other hand—the one made of stone, so remote, so out of place there in the sky on the end of its rope; the others made of flesh, so bursting with life. Nobody in the audience was in any doubt as to which of the two came out ahead or at whose expense the laughter was. But then the helicopter continues on its way, and the great dome of St. Peter's looms up from below, and for the first time the camera starts to zoom in on the statue itself with its arms stretched out, until for a moment the screen is almost filled with just the bearded face of Christ—and at that moment there was no laughter at all in that theater full of students and their dates and paper cups full of buttery popcorn and La Dolce Vita college-style. Nobody laughed during that moment because there was something about that face, for a few seconds there on the screen, that made them be silent—the face hovering there in the sky and the outspread arms. For a moment, not very long to be sure, there was no sound, as if the face were their face some-how, their secret face that they had never seen before but that they knew belonged to them, or the face that they had never seen before but that they knew, if only for a moment, they belonged to.

I think that is much of what the Christian faith is. It is for a moment, just for a little while, seeing the face and being still; that is all. There is so much about the whole religious enterprise that seems superannuated and irrelevant and as out of place in our age as an antique statue is out of place in the sky. But just for the moment itself, say, of Christmas, there can be only silence as something comes to life, some spirit, some hope; as something is born again into the world that is so strange and new and precious that not even a cynic can laugh although he might be tempted to weep.

The face in the sky. The child born in the night among beasts. The sweet breath and steaming dung of beasts. And nothing is ever the same again.

Those who believe in God can never in a way be sure of him again. Once they have seen him in a stable, they can never be sure where he will appear or to what lengths he will go or to what ludicrous depths of self-humiliation he will descend in his wild pursuit of man. If holiness and the awful power and majesty of God were present in this least auspi-cious of all events, this birth of a peasant's child, then there is no place or time so lowly and earthbound but that holiness can be present there too. And this means that we are never safe, that there is no place where we can hide from God, no place where we are safe from his power to break in two and re-create the human heart because it is just where he seems most helpless that he is most strong, and just where we least expect him that he comes most fully.

For those who believe in God, it means, this birth, that God himself is never safe from us, and maybe that is the dark side of Christmas, the terror of the silence. He comes in such a way that we can always turn him down, as we could crack the baby's skull like an eggshell or nail him up when he gets too big for that. God comes to us in the hungry man we do not have to feed, comes to us in the lonely man we do not have to comfort, comes to us in all the desperate human need of people everywhere that we are always free to turn our backs upon. It means that God puts himself at our mercy not only in the sense of the suffering that we can cause him by our blindness and coldness and cruelty, but the suffering that we can cause him simply by suffering ourselves. Because that is the way love works, and when someone we love suffers, we suffer with him, and we would not have it otherwise be-cause the suffering and the love are one, just as it is with God's love for us.

The child is born in the night—the mother's exhausted flesh, the father's face clenched like a fist—and nothing is ever the same again. Nothing is ever the same again for those who believe in God, and nothing is ever the same again for those who do not believe in God either, because once the birth has happened, it is no longer just God whom they have to deny but it is also this event that they have to deny. Those who do not believe must also fall silent in the presence of the new-born child, but their silence can have only tears at its heart because for them this can only be another child born to die as every child is born to die, and no matter how bravely and well he lives it, his life can have no meaning beyond the meaning that he gives it, and then like all life it must be like a dream once it has been dreamed. For those who do not believe, all the great poetry of the birth—the angels, the star, the three kings coming out of the night to lay their gifts in the straw—can be only like words which for all their beauty are written on the sand, not poetry that points beyond itself to the very heart of reality, which is beyond the power of time and change to touch.

But what of those who both believe and do not believe, cannot believe—which is some men all of the time and all men some of the time? The statue with its outstretched arms hovers in the sky, the still face looks down, and they recognize the face and call its name. They wave and go running a little way along the uneven ground beneath it. The night deepens and grows still, and maybe the only sound is the birth-cry, the little agony of new life coming alive, or maybe there is also the sound of legions of unseen voices raised in joy.

For them too, the believing unbelievers, nothing is ever quite the same again either, because what they have seen and heard in that moment of stillness is, just possibly, possibly, the hope of the world. And what they feel in their hearts as they wave—maybe only with one hand, a little wave, not very certain but with his name on their lips—is the stirring of new life, new courage, new gladness seeking to be born in them even as he is born, if only they too, we too, the wide world too, will stretch out our arms to those arms and raise our empty faces to that bewildering face.

L O R D Jesus Christ,
Thou Son of the Most High, Prince of Peace, be born again into our world. Wherever there is war in this world, wherever there is pain, wherever there is loneliness, wherever there is no hope, come, thou long-expected one, with healing in thy wings.

Holy Child, whom the shepherds and the kings and the dumb beasts adored, be born again. Wherever there is boredom, wherever there is fear of failure, wherever there is temptation too strong to resist, wherever there is bitterness of heart, come, thou blessed one, with healing in thy wings.

Saviour, be born in each of us who raises his face to thy face, not knowing fully who he is or who thou art, knowing only that thy love is beyond his knowing and that no other has the power to make him whole. Come, Lord Jesus, to each who longs for thee even though he has forgotten thy name. Come quickly. *Amen.*

2

Confusion of Face

In the first year of Darius the son of Ahasuerus, by birth a Mede, who became king over the realm of the Chaldeans—in the first year of his reign, I, Daniel, perceived in the books the number of years which, according to the word of the Lord to Jeremiah the prophet, must pass before the end of the desolations of Jerusalem, namely, seventy years.

Then I turned my face to the Lord God, seeking him by prayer and supplications with fasting and sackcloth and ashes. I prayed to the Lord my God and made confession, saying, "O Lord, the great and terrible God, who keepest covenant and steadfast love with those who love him and keep his commandments, we have sinned and done wrong and acted wickedly and rebelled, turning aside from thy commandments and ordinances; we have not listened to thy servants the prophets, who spoke in thy name to our kings, our princes, and our fathers, and to all the people of the land. To thee, O Lord, belongs righteousness, but to us confusion of face, as at this day, to the men of Judah, to the inhabitants of Jerusalem, and to all Israel, those that are near and those that are far away, in all the lands to which thou hast driven them, because of the treachery which they have committed against thee. To us, O Lord, belongs confusion of face, to our kings, to our princes, and to our fathers, because we have sinned against thee. DANIEL 9:1–8

The author of the Book of Daniel, whoever he was, lists in a general way all the sins of his nation: "We have done wrong," he says, "and acted wickedly and rebelled, and turned aside from the commandments of God and not listened to the prophets"—all these familiar words of prophetic denunciation—and for that reason, he says, in words that all of a sudden become unfamiliar, "to us belongs confusion of face." It is a strange phrase, but it is also a just one. Confusion of face is somehow the truth of it. Because faces are confusing, that is all. The preacher looks out at the faces of his congregation, and he is confused. He sees expressions in those faces of attention and inattention, of vague expectancy and glazed resignation, and he wonders what is going on behind those faces. And it strikes him that as they look up at his face and ask themselves the same question about him, they might do well to be confused too: Is his heart really in what he is saying, or is he saying only what he thinks they expect a preacher to say? And if his heart is not in what he is saying, then what is his heart in? And if his heart is in what he is saying, then what about the remainder of his heart, because surely he is not saying all that is in it, nor would he, nor could he even if he wanted to. And to go just one step further down this road of confusion, it is not just that their faces confuse him and that his, if they stop to think of it, should confuse them; but he is often confused by his own face, and he would not be likely to admit this if he were not quite certain that all men are often confused by their own faces too.

There is a silly little jingle that goes something like this:

My face I don't mind it
For I am behind it,
It's the people out front get the jar.

But, on the contrary, the person inside gets the jar too. You catch sight of your face in the mirror when you are brushing your teeth in the morning or combing your hair, and often you say, in effect, "Well, there it is again, the same old washed and slept-on thing I saw yesterday and will see again tomorrow—no better and no worse." But sometimes, I believe, there is another response which is deeply jarring and which involves your asking in effect, "Is that really me? Am I my face?" And although the answer of course is Yes, the answer of course is also No. I am my face, and I am not. A strange and confusing business.

Beneath the face there are many layers of self, and the deepest layers are for the most part hidden from us. You read a letter that you wrote or you remember something that you said or did, maybe even as recently as yesterday, and you think, "How could I ever have written such a thing, said such a thing? Is that even who I once was, let alone who I am now?" And because of the way the world goes, the sad truth seems to be that the face that you disclaim responsibility for is more often than not apt to be worse than the person you feel that you know yourself to be beneath the face. There is a self beneath the self, and the language that the inner self speaks could well be the language of St. Paul when he wrote to the church at Rome: "I do not understand my own actions. For I do not do what I want, but I do the very thing I hate." In other words, I am confused by my own face. Poor Paul. Poor all of us.

THE SEARCH

The world has a face too, of course, the world of history. Most of the time we avoid looking at it, really looking, for fear of being turned to stone. But once in a while, we are forced into looking. Things happen that will not let us *not* look, different things for different people. After one of our air strikes against North Vietnam, the Viet Cong was reported to have gone into a village and killed ninety children in retaliation. Most of the time you read these things the way you read a work of fiction; in some remote way you know that it is terrible. But sometimes the face of the world becomes so contorted, its expression so agonized, that it catches your eye in spite of yourself; and the face of the world becomes suddenly the putty-colored face of just one of those dead children. And the way that well-fed, fat-rumped people like you and me live most of our lives, unmoved by such agony, that becomes the face of the world too. At such times we say once again, not just about our own faces now but about the world's bloody face, "Is this really what the world is—this obscenity? Is this really the face of humanity?" Yes, it is, God help us. No, it is not. Confusion of face, a confusion that feels like nausea. Enough of this.

There is a poem by a Japanese poet named Yagi Jūkichi, about whom I know nothing except for this:

> I first saw my face in a dream
>> on a night when my fever had been high
>> for some time.
> I had gone to sleep praying to Christ
>> and a face was revealed.
> Not, of course, my face nowadays
>> nor my face when I was young
>> nor the face of the noblest of angels
>> as I always picture it in my mind.

It was a face surpassing even this—
And I knew at once it was my own.

About the face was a gold-tinged blackness.
The next day when my eyes opened
The fever raged no less,
But in my heart was a strange calm.

Who is that person over there—you, me, whoever he is?
Well, there are really two of him. There is the him everybody
knows, the him you see around, very cool, very this, very
that. And then there is the other him, the real him, that not
many people know. Very few. And maybe beneath that there
is another him too, and beneath that? Beneath that . . . .

"Look now. As a nation or as an individual, you get what
you fight for in this world, and if you don't fight for it, nobody's going to hand it to you on a silver platter. If you
don't fight, people are going to walk all over you—any fool
knows that. If you want to get ahead, you better start push-
ing ahead. Certainly you're going to have to step on a few
people's toes, people are going to get hurt. But you can't be
everybody's friend, business is business, war is war. It's a
hard world."

This is the face that each of us wears in some measure.
It is a face that we know well: something a little remote
about the eyes; the line of the jaw a little hard; disguise it as
we will, the expression is at best indifferent or vaguely
troubled, at worst pitiless, as we look out at the suffering and
need of the people around us. It is a face that in part we
choose to protect ourselves from the world by. It is a face
that in part the world chooses for us, perhaps to protect itself
by. And it is a confusing face just because there are other

layers of self beneath it. There is the conscience, for instance, the inner voice which says that the face I wear is not the face I ought to wear; it is wrong somehow to be indifferent, pitiless, afraid—the face of the world is wrong, my face. But beneath the conscience, the sense of guilt, there is a much deeper level: not just that I ought not to be what at my worst I appear but that I do not really want to be. I fend off the world, I avoid getting involved with other people's needs, so that I can get ahead in the world myself. But at this deeper level, much deeper than conscience, the truth of it is that I need the world. I need the very ones that I keep at a distance. I need to love and be loved by the very ones from whom I hide myself behind this face. I need them not so that I can ease my conscience but so that I can be myself.

Fathoms down into the mystery of yourself you go—into the darkness of guilt and beyond, into the darkness of loneliness and need and beyond. Deeper and deeper you go until at last the darkness begins to be tinged with gold, as the poem says, which is the gold of light. And in that light you begin to see, as in a dream at first, your own true face. "Not my face nowadays, nor my face when I was young, nor the face of the noblest of angels," but a face that surpasses all these because it is the face of love, a face like Christ's. Words like these are in many ways unpopular and distasteful in our culture; they deal with introspection and self-examination, and we tend to shy away from such enterprises because they seem somehow unhealthy and morbid, because they lead us away from action, and we are all activists. If we are not doing something, we feel guilty, and we keep on doing, doing, as a way to avoid thinking. We shy away from introspection because, however fearful the surface seems, we fear the depths still more. And we are right; there is much to fear there.

The voyage into the self is long and dark and full of peril, but I believe that it is a voyage that all of us will have to make before we are through. Either we climb down into the abyss willingly with our eyes open, or we risk falling into it with our eyes closed—a point on which religion and psychiatry seem to agree. And I believe that what is said in the language of the Japanese poem is true also in the language of fact; that if we search ourselves deeply enough, we will begin to see at last who we really are, we will begin to see, very dimly at first, our own true faces. And then, although on the surface the fever may rage still, I believe that a strange calm does begin to come, a peace that passes understanding.

Selfhood in the sense that you are one self and I am another self begins to fade. You begin to understand that in some way your deepest self is the self of all men—that you are in them and they are in you. You begin to understand not as an ideal but as a reality, an experience, that their pain is your pain, their need your need; that there can really be no getting ahead at their expense, there can be no joy for you until there is joy for them. And whatever your religion is, or your lack of religion, in this sense I think that the soul of every man is Christian and that the man on the cross who finds peace and fullness and true life is at the very least a symbol of the deepest truth about every one of us. I believe that by God's grace it is our destiny, in this life or in whatever life awaits us, to discover the face of our inmost being, to become at last and at great cost who we truly are.

Thou God in Christ,
There is no ground anywhere that is not holy
ground, for in the cool of the evening thou hast walked upon
it and in the heat of the day thou hast died upon it, and at the
coming of dawn thou hast returned and art always and everywhere returning to it and to us who walk upon it too, this
holy ground, though heedless of its holiness. O make us
whole. Set us free.

Thou didst shape us each in the darkness of a womb to
give us life and thou knowest us each by name, and not one
is forgotten by thee, not one but is precious in thy sight—
the ugly with the beautiful, the criminal with the child, the
enemy with the friend. Lord, give us eyes to see each other
and ourselves more nearly as thou seest us, to see beneath
each face we meet, and beneath even our own faces, thy face.

Help us to know that for each thou hast died as though
he were the only one. *Amen.*

3

The Calling of Voices

In the year that King Uzziah died I saw the Lord sitting upon a throne, high and lifted up; and his train filled the temple. Above him stood the seraphim; each had six wings: with two he covered his face, and with two he covered his feet, and with two he flew. And one called to another and said:

"Holy, holy, holy is the Lord of hosts;
the whole earth is full of his glory."

And the foundations of the thresholds shook at the voice of him who called, and the house was filled with smoke. And I said: "Woe is me! For I am lost; for I am a man of unclean lips, and I dwell in the midst of a people of unclean lips; for my eyes have seen the King, the Lord of hosts!"

Then flew one of the seraphim to me, having in his hand a burning coal which he had taken with tongs from the altar. And he touched my mouth, and said: "Behold, this has touched your lips; your guilt is taken away, and your sin forgiven." And I heard the voice of the Lord saying, "Whom shall I send, and who will go for us?" Then I said, "Here I am! Send me." And he said, "Go. . . ."   ISAIAH 6: 1–9

"Man shall not live by bread alone,
but by every word that proceeds from the mouth of God."
                                               MATTHEW 4:4

The telephone rings late one night, and you jump out of your skin; you try for a while to pretend that it is not ringing, but after a while you answer it because otherwise you will never know who it is, and it might be anybody, anybody. Then a voice says, "Listen, something has happened. Something has got to be done. I know you are busy. I know you have lots on your mind. But you've got to come. For God's sake."

Or you are walking along an empty beach toward the end of the day, and there is a gray wind blowing, and a seagull with a mussel shell in its beak flaps up and up, and then lets the shell drop to the rocks below, and there is something so wild and brave and beautiful about it that you have to write it into a poem or paint it into a picture or sing it into a song; or if you are no good at any of these, you have to live out at least the rest of that day in a way that is somehow true to the little scrap of wonder that you have seen.

Or I think of the school church that I served for a time where the offering each week was given to an institution for retarded children, and when the plate was passed around, some of the students, resentful of having to go to church at all, would drop in their penny or would drop in nothing at all. Then maybe someday a friend would drag one of them down to where the money went, and he would get to know some one of the children a little, and when he went back another day, the child would come running up to him in a way that made him suddenly see, with a kind of panic almost, that for that child, the sight of him was Christmas morning and a rocket to the moon and the no-school whistle on a snowy morning. And then it was like the phone ringing in the night again or the seagull riding the gray wind. It was a summons that he had to answer somehow or, at considerable cost, not answer.

Or in the year that King Uzziah died, or in the year that John F. Kennedy died, or in the year that somebody you loved died, you go into the temple if that is your taste, or you hide your face in the little padded temple of your hands, and a voice says, "Whom shall I send into the pain of a world where people die?" and if you are not careful, you may find yourself answering, "Send me." You may hear the voice say, "Go." Just *go*.

Like "duty," "law," "religion," the word "vocation" has a dull ring to it, but in terms of what it means, it is really not dull at all. *Vocare*, to call, of course, and a man's vocation is a man's calling. It is the work that he is called to in this world, the thing that he is summoned to spend his life doing. We can speak of a man's choosing his vocation, but perhaps it is at least as accurate to speak of a vocation's choosing the man, of a call's being given and a man's hearing it, or not hearing it. And maybe that is the place to start: the business of listening and hearing. A man's life is full of all sorts of voices calling him in all sorts of directions. Some of them are voices from inside and some of them are voices from outside. The more alive and alert we are, the more clamorous our lives are. Which do we listen to? What kind of voice do we listen for?

There is a sad and dangerous little game that people play when they get to be a certain age. It is a form of solitaire. They get out their class yearbook, and look at the pictures of the classmates they knew best and recall the days when they first knew them in school, ten or twenty years ago or whatever it was. They think about all the exciting, crazy, wonderfully characteristic things their classmates used to be interested in and about the kind of dreams they had about what they were going to do when they graduated and about the kind of dreams that maybe they had for some of them. Then they think about what those classmates actually did with their lives, what they are doing with them now ten or twenty years later. I make no claim that the game is always sad or that when it seems to be sad our judgment is always right, but once or twice when I have played it myself, sadness has been a large part of what I have felt. Because in my class, at the school that I went to, as in any class at any school, there were students who had a real flair, a real talent, for something. Maybe it was for writing or acting or sports. Maybe it was an interest and a joy in working with people toward some common goal, a sense of responsibility for people who in some way had less than they had or were less. Sometimes it was just their capacity for being so alive that made you more alive to be with them. Yet now, a good many years later, I have the feeling that more than just a few of them are spending their lives at work in which none of these gifts is being used, at work they seem to be working at with neither much pleasure nor any sense of accomplishment. This is the sadness of the game, and the danger of it is that maybe we find that in some measure we are among them or that we are too blind to see that we are.

When you are young, I think, your hearing is in some ways better than it is ever going to be again. You hear better than most people the voices that call to you out of your own life to give yourself to this work or that work. When you are young, before you accumulate responsibilities, you are freer than most people to choose among all the voices and to answer the one that speaks most powerfully to who you are and to what you really want to do with your life. But the danger is that there are so many voices, and they all in their ways sound so promising. The danger is that you will not listen to the voice that speaks to you through the seagull mounting the gray wind, say, or the vision in the temple, that you do not listen to the voice inside you or to the voice that speaks from outside but specifically to you out of the specific events of your life, but that instead you listen to the great blaring, boring, banal voice of our mass culture, which threatens to deafen us all by blasting forth that the only thing that really matters about your work is how much it will get you in the way of salary and status, and that if it is gladness you are after, you can save that for weekends. In fact one of the grimmer notions that we seem to inherit from our Puritan forebears is that work is not even supposed to be glad but, rather, a kind of penance, a way of working off the guilt that you accumulate during the hours when you are not working.

The world is full of people who seem to have listened to the wrong voice and are now engaged in life-work in which they find no pleasure or purpose and who run the risk of suddenly realizing someday that they have spent the only years that they are ever going to get in this world doing something which could not matter less to themselves or to anyone else. This does not mean, of course, people who are doing work that from the outside looks unglamorous and humdrum, because obviously such work as that may be a crucial form of service and deeply creative. But it means people who are doing work that seems simply irrelevant not only to the great human needs and issues of our time but also to their own need to grow and develop as humans.

In John Marquand's novel *Point of No Return*, for instance, after years of apple-polishing and bucking for promotion and dedicating all his energies to a single goal, Charlie Gray finally gets to be vice-president of the fancy little New York bank where he works; and then the terrible moment comes when he realizes that it is really not what he wanted after all, when the prize that he has spent his life trying to win suddenly turns to ashes in his hands. His promotion assures him and his family of all the security and standing that he has always sought, but Marquand leaves you with the feeling that maybe the best way Charlie Gray could have supported his family would have been by giving his life to the kind of work where he could have expressed himself and fulfilled himself in such a way as to become in himself, as a person, the kind of support they really needed.

There is also the moment in the Gospels where Jesus is portrayed as going into the wilderness for forty days and nights and being tempted there by the devil. And one of the ways that the devil tempts him is to wait until Jesus is very hungry from fasting and then to suggest that he simply turn the stones into bread and eat. Jesus answers, "Man shall not live by bread alone," and this just happens to be, among other things, true, and very close to the same truth that Charlie Gray comes to when he realizes too late that he was not made to live on status and salary alone but that something crucially important was missing from his life even though he was not sure what it was any more than, perhaps, Marquand himself was sure what it was.

There is nothing moralistic or sentimental about this truth. It means for us simply that we must be careful with our lives, for Christ's sake, because it would seem that they are the only lives we are going to have in this puzzling and perilous world, and so they are very precious and what we do with them matters enormously. Everybody knows that. We need no one to tell it to us. Yet in another way perhaps we do always need to be told, because there is always the temptation to believe that we have all the time in the world, whereas the truth of it is that we do not. We have only a life, and the choice of how we are going to live it must be our own choice, not one that we let the world make for us. Because surely Marquand was right that for each of us there comes a point of no return, a point beyond which we no longer have life enough left to go back and start all over again.

To Isaiah, the voice said, "Go," and for each of us there are many voices that say it, but the question is which one will we obey with our lives, which of the voices that call is to be the one that we answer. No one can say, of course, except each for himself, but I believe that it is possible to say at least this in general to all of us: we should go with our lives where we most need to go and where we are most needed.

Where we most need to go. Maybe that means that the voice we should listen to most as we choose a vocation is the voice that we might think we should listen to least, and that is the voice of our own gladness. What can we do that makes us gladdest, what can we do that leaves us with the strongest sense of sailing true north and of peace, which is much of what gladness is? Is it making things with our hands out of wood or stone or paint on canvas? Or is it making something we hope like truth out of words? Or is it making people laugh or weep in a way that cleanses their spirit? I believe that if it is a thing that makes us truly glad, then it is a good thing and it is our thing and it is the calling voice that we were made to answer with our lives.

And also, where we are most needed. In a world where there is so much drudgery, so much grief, so much emptiness and fear and pain, our gladness in our work is as much needed as we ourselves need to be glad. If we keep our eyes and ears open, our hearts open, we will find the place surely. The phone will ring and we will jump not so much out of our skin as into our skin. If we keep our lives open, the right place will find us.

Jesus said, "Man shall not live by bread alone, but by every word that proceeds from the mouth of God," and in the end every word that proceeds from the mouth of God is the same word, and the word is Christ himself. And in the end that is the vocation, the calling of all of us, the calling to be Christs. To be Christs in whatever way we are able to be. To be Christs with whatever gladness we have and in whatever place, among whatever brothers we are called to. That is the vocation, the destiny to which we were all of us called even before the foundations of the world.

O THOU,
Who art the God no less of those who know thee not than of those who love thee well, be present with us at the times of choosing when time stands still and all that lies behind and all that lies ahead are caught up in the mystery of

a moment. Be present especially with the young who must choose between many voices. Help them to know how much an old world needs their youth and gladness. Help them to know that there are words of truth and healing that will never be spoken unless they speak them, and deeds of compassion and courage that will never be done unless they do them. Help them never to mistake success for victory or failure for defeat. Grant that they may never be entirely content with whatever bounty the world may bestow upon them, but that they may know at last that they were created not for happiness but for joy, and that joy is to him alone who, sometimes with tears in his eyes, commits himself in love to thee and to his brothers. Lead them and all thy world ever deeper into the knowledge that finally all men are one and that there can never really be joy for any until there is joy for all. In Christ's name we ask it and for his sake. *Amen.*

4

A Sprig of Hope

Now the earth was corrupt in God's sight, and the earth was filled with violence. And God saw the earth, and behold, it was corrupt; for all flesh had corrupted their way upon the earth. And God said to Noah, "I have determined to make an end of all flesh; for the earth is filled with violence through them; . . . behold, I will bring a flood of waters upon the earth, to destroy all flesh in which is the breath of life. . . . Make yourself an ark of gopher wood; make rooms in the ark, and cover it inside and out with pitch. . . . And of every living thing of all flesh, you shall bring two of every sort into the ark, to keep them alive with you; they shall be male and female. . . . For in seven days I will send rain upon the earth forty days and forty nights; and every living thing that I have made I will blot out from the face of the ground." And Noah did all that the Lord had commanded him. . . .

In the sixth hundredth year of Noah's life, in the second month, on the seventeenth day of the month, on that day all the fountains of the great deep burst forth, and the windows of the heavens were opened. . . .

The flood continued forty days upon the earth; and the waters increased, and bore up the ark, and it rose high above the earth. The waters prevailed and increased greatly upon the earth; and the ark floated on the face of the waters. And the waters prevailed so mightily upon the earth that all the high mountains under the whole heaven were covered . . .

fifteen cubits deep. . . . Only Noah was left, and those that
were with him in the ark. . . .

At the end of forty days Noah opened the window of
the ark which he had made, . . .

Then he sent forth a dove from him, to see if the waters
had subsided from the face of the ground; but the dove found
no place to set her foot, and she returned to him to the ark,
for the waters were still on the face of the whole earth. So he
put forth his hand . . . and brought her into the ark with
him. He waited another seven days, and again he sent forth
the dove out of the ark; and the dove came back to him in
the evening, and lo, in her mouth a freshly plucked olive leaf.

GENESIS 6:11–8:11, PASSIM

It is an ironic fact that this ancient legend about Noah
survives in our age mainly as a children's story. When I
was a child, I had a Noah's ark made of wood with a roof
that came off so you could take the animals out and put them
in again, and my children have one too; yet if you stop to
look at it at all, this is really as dark a tale as there is in the
Bible, which is full of dark tales. It is a tale of God's terrible
despair over the human race and his decision to visit them
with a great flood that would destroy them all except for
this one old man, Noah, and his family. Only now we give
it to children to read. One wonders why.

Not, I suspect, because children particularly want to
read it, but more because their elders particularly do not
want to read it or at least do not want to read it for what it
actually says and so make it instead into a fairy tale, which
no one has to take seriously—just the way we make black
jokes about disease and death so that we can laugh instead of

weep at them; just the way we translate murder and lust into sixth-rate television melodramas, which is to reduce them to a size that anybody can cope with; just the way we take the nightmares of our age, the sinister, brutal forces that dwell in the human heart threatening always to overwhelm us, and present them as the Addams family or the monster dolls that we give, again, to children. *Gulliver's Travels* is too bitter about man, so we make it into an animated cartoon; *Moby Dick* is too bitter about God, so we make it into an adventure story for boys; Noah's ark is too something-or-other else, so it becomes a toy with a roof that comes off so you can take the little animals out. This is one way of dealing with the harsher realities of our existence, and since the alternative is, by facing them head on, to risk adding more to our burden of anxiety than we are able to bear, it may not be such a bad 'way at that. But for all our stratagems, the legends, the myths, persist among us, and even in the guise of fairy tales for the young they continue to embody truths or intuitions which in the long run it is perhaps more dangerous to evade than to confront.

So, what then are the truths embodied in this tale of Noah and his ark? Let us start with the story itself, more particularly let us start with the moment when God first spoke to Noah, more particularly let us start with Noah's face at that moment when God first spoke to him.

When somebody speaks to you, you turn your face to look in the direction that the voice comes from; but if the voice comes from no direction at all, if the voice comes from within and comes wordlessly, and more powerfully for being wordless, then in a sense you stop looking at anything at all. Your eyes become unseeing, and if someone were to pass his hand in front of them, you would hardly notice the hand. If you can be said to be looking at anything then, you are probably looking at, without really seeing, something of no importance whatever like the branch of a tree stirring in the wind or the frayed cuff of your shirt where your arm rests on the windowsill. Your face goes vacant because for the moment you have vacated it and are living somewhere beneath your face, wherever it is that the voice comes from. So it was maybe with Noah's face when he heard the words that he heard, or when he heard what he heard translated clumsily into words: that the earth was corrupt in God's sight, filled with violence and pain and unlove—that the earth was doomed.

It was presumably nothing that Noah had not known already, nothing that any man who has ever lived on this earth with his eyes open has not known. But because it came upon him, sudden and strong, he had to face it more squarely than people usually do, and it rose up in him like a pain in his own belly. And then maybe, like Kierkegaard's Abraham, Noah asked whether it was God who was speaking or only the pain in his belly; whether it was a vision of the glory of the world as it first emerged from the hand of the Creator that led him to the knowledge of how far the world had fallen, or whether it was just his pathetic human longing for a glory that had never been and would never be. If that was his question, perhaps a flicker of bewilderment passed across his vacant face—the lines between his eyes deepening, his mouth going loose, a little stupid. A penny for your thoughts, old Noah.

But then came the crux of the thing because the voice that was either God's voice or an undigested matzoh ball shifted from the indicative of doom to the imperative of command and it told him that although the world was doomed, he, Noah, had a commission to perform that would have much to do with the saving of the world. "Make yourself an ark of gopher wood," the voice said, "and behold, I will bring a flood of waters upon the earth to destroy all flesh in which is the breath of life." So Noah had to decide, and the decision was not just a theological one—yes, it is God; no, it is not; and you live your life the same way in either case—because if the voice proceeded not from the mystery of the human belly but from the mystery and depth of life itself, then Noah had to obey, and Noah knew it; and out of common humanity this is the point to shift our gaze from his face because things are happening there that no stranger should be allowed to see, and to look instead at his feet because when a man has to decide which way he is going to bet his entire life, it is very often the feet that finally tell the tale.

There are Noah's feet—dusty, a little slew-footed, Chaplinesque, stock still. You watch them. Even the birds in the trees watch. Which direction will the feet move, or will they move at all? It comes down to that with every man finally. And finally they do move. Maybe with no spring in the step, maybe dragging a little, but they move nevertheless. And they move in the direction of . . . the lumber yard . . . as he bets his life on his voice.

There are so many things to say about Noah, whoever he was, if ever he was, the old landlubber with the watery, watery eyes; but the one thing that is certain is that he must have looked like an awful fool for a while, for all those days it took him to knock together the great and ponderous craft.

Three hundred cubits long and fifty cubits wide and thirty cubits high, all three decks of it covered inside and out with pitch, and he had nothing more plausible in the way of an explanation than that he was building it—and building it many a mile from the nearest port—because a voice had told him to, which was maybe God's voice or maybe hardening of the arteries. Only a fool would heed such a voice at all when every other voice for miles around could tell him, and probably did, that the proper business of a man is to keep busy: to work, to play, to make love, to watch out for his own interests as all men watch out for theirs, and to leave the whole shadowy business of God to those who have a taste for shadows. So Noah building his ark becomes the bearded joke draped in a sheet who walks down Broadway with his sandwich-board inscribed REPENT; and Noah's face becomes the great white moonface of the clown looking up with anguish at the ones who act out their dance of death on the high-wire. A penny for your thoughts, old Noah, as you pound together your zany craft while the world goes about its business as usual and there is not a cloud in the sky.

His thoughts, one imagines, were of water, and as the windows of heaven were opened and all the fountains of the great deep burst forth so that the sea crept in over the earth, and where there had been dry land and order all was disorder and violence, perhaps Noah knew that it had always been so. Perhaps Noah knew that all the order and busy-ness of men had been at best an illusion and that, left to himself, man had always been doomed. The waters came scudding in over forest and field, sliding in across kitchen floors and down cellar stairs, rising high above television aerials and the steeples of churches, and death was everywhere as death is always everywhere, men trapped alone as they are always trapped, always alone, in office or locker room, bedroom or bar, men grasping out for something solid and sure to keep themselves from drowning, brother fighting brother for the few remaining pieces of dry ground. Maybe the chaos was no greater than it has ever been. Only wetter.

The ark rose free from its moorings, cumbersome old tub creaking and pitching in the wilderness of waves with the two of everything down below and a clown for a captain who did not know his port from his starboard. But it stayed afloat, by God, this Toonerville trolley of vessels, clouted from side to side by the waves and staggering like a drunk. It was not much, God knows, but it was enough, and it stayed afloat, and granted that it was noisy as Hell and stank to Heaven, creatures took comfort from each other's creatureliness, and the wolf lay down with the lamb, and the lion ate straw like the ox, and life lived on in the ark while all around there was only chaos and death.

Then finally, after many days, Noah sent forth a dove from the ark to see if the waters had subsided from the earth, and that evening she returned, and lo, in her mouth a freshly plucked olive leaf. Once again, for the last time, the place to look, I think, is Noah's face. The dove stands there with her delicate, scarlet feet on the calluses of his upturned palm. His cheek just touches her breast so that he can feel the tiny panic of her heart. His eyes are closed, the lashes watery wet. Only what he weeps with now, the old clown, is no longer anguish but wild and irrepressible hope. That is not the end of the story in Genesis, but maybe that is the end of it for most of us—just a little sprig of hope held up against the end of the world.

All these old tales are about us, of course, and I suppose that is why we can never altogether forget them; that is why, even if we do not read them any more ourselves, we give them to children to read so that they will never be entirely lost, because if they were, part of the truth about us would be lost too. The truth, for instance, that, left to ourselves, as a race we *are* doomed—what else can we conclude?—doomed if only by our own insatiable lust for doom. Despair and destruction and death are the ancient enemies, and yet we are always so helplessly drawn to them that it is as if we are more than half in love with our enemies. Even our noblest impulses and purest dreams get all tangled up with them just as in Vietnam, in the name of human dignity and freedom, the bombs are falling on both the just and the unjust and we recoil at the horror of little children with their faces burned off, except that somehow that is the way the world has always been and is, with nightmare and noble dream all tangled up together. That is the way we are doomed—doomed to be what we are, doomed to seek our own doom. And the turbulent waters of chaos and nightmare are always threatening to burst forth and flood the earth. We hardly need the tale of Noah to tell us that. *The New York Times* tells us just as well, and our own hearts tell us well too, because chaos and nightmare have their little days there also. But the tale of Noah tells other truths as well.

It tells about the ark, for one, which somehow managed to ride out the storm. God knows the ark is not much—if anybody knows it is not much, God knows—and the old joke seems true that if it were not for the storm without, you could never stand the stench within. But the ark was enough, is enough. Because the ark is wherever human beings come together as human beings in such a way that the differences between them stop being barriers—the way, if people meet at the wedding, say, of someone they both love, all the differences of age between them, all the real and imagined differences of color, of wealth, of education, no longer divide them but become for each a source of strength and delight, and although they may go right on looking at each other as very odd fish indeed, it becomes an oddness to gladden the heart, and there is no shyness any more, no awkwardness or fear of each other. Sometimes even in a church we can look into each other's faces and see that, beneath the differences, we are all of us outward bound on a voyage for parts unknown.

The ark is wherever people come together because this is a stormy world where nothing stays put for long among the crazy waves and where at the end of every voyage there is a burial at sea. The ark is where, just because it is such a world, we really need each other and know very well that we do. The ark is wherever human beings come together because in their heart of hearts all of them—white and black, Russian and American, hippie and square—dream the same dream, which is a dream of peace—peace between the nations, between the races, between the brothers—and thus ultimately a dream of love. Love, not as an excuse for the mushy and innocuous, but love as a summons to battle against all that is unlovely and unloving in the world. The ark, in other words, is where we have each other and where we have hope.

Noah looked like a fool in his faith, but he saved the world from drowning, and we must not forget the one whom Noah foreshadows and who also looked like a fool spread-eagled up there, cross-eyed with pain, but who also saved the world from drowning. We must not forget him because he saves the world still, and wherever the ark is, wherever we meet and touch in something like love, it is because he also is there, brother and father of us all. So into his gracious and puzzling hands we must commend ourselves through all the days of our voyaging wherever it takes us, and at the end of all our voyages. We must build our arks with love and ride out the storm with courage and know that the little sprig of green in the dove's mouth betokens a reality beyond the storm more precious than the likes of us can imagine.

H o w can we pray to thee, thou holy and hidden God, whose ways are not our ways, who reignest in awful mystery beyond the realm of space and time? Yet how can we not pray to thee, Heavenly Father, who knowest what it is to be a man because thou hast walked among us as a man, breaking with us the bread of our affliction and drinking deep of the cup of our despair? How can we not pray to thee when it is thy very Spirit alive within us that moves our lips in prayer?

Hear, O God, the prayers of all thy children everywhere: for forgiveness and healing, for courage, for faith; prayers for the needs of others; prayers for peace among the desperate nations. Whether thou givest or withholdest what we ask, whether thou answerest us in words that burn like fire or in silence that burns like fire, increase in us the knowledge that thou art always more near to us than breathing, that thy will for us is love.

And deep beneath all our asking, so deep beneath that

44

we are all but deaf to it ourselves, hear, O God, the secret
song of every human heart praising thee for being what thou
art, rejoicing with the morning stars that thou art our God
and we thy children. Make strong and wild this secret song
within until it bursts forth at last to thy glory and our saving.
Through Jesus Christ our Lord.   *Amen.*

5

Pontifex

He has put my brethren far from me,
  and my acquaintances are wholly estranged from me.
My kinsfolk and my close friends have failed me;
  the guests in my house have forgotten me; . . .
I have become an alien in their eyes.

JOB 19:13–15

"No man is an Island," Dr. Donne wrote, "intire of it selfe; every man is a peece of the Continent, a part of the maine; if a Clod be washed away by the Sea, Europe is the lesse, as well as if a Promontorie were, as well as if a Mannor of thy friends or of thine owne were; any mans death diminishes me, because I am involved in Mankinde; And therefore never send to know for whom the bell tolls; It tolls for thee."

Or to use another metaphor, humanity is like an enormous spider web, so that if you touch it anywhere, you set the whole thing trembling. Sometime during the extraordinary week that followed the assassination of John F. Kennedy in Dallas, the newspapers carried the story that when that crusty old warhorse, Andrei Gromyko, signed the memorial volume at the United States embassy in Moscow, there were tears in his eyes; and I do not think that you have to be either naïve or sentimental to believe that they were real tears. Surely it was not that the Soviet Foreign Minister had any love for the young American President, but that he recognized that in some sense every man was diminished by that man's death. In some sense I believe that the death of Kennedy was a kind of death for his enemies no less than for his countrymen. Just as John Donne believed that any man's death, when we are confronted by it, reminds us of our common destiny as human beings: to be born, to live, to struggle a while, and finally to die. We are all of us in it together.

Nor does it need anything as cataclysmic as the death of a President to remind us of this. As we move around this world and as we act with kindness, perhaps, or with indifference, or with hostility, toward the people we meet, we too are setting the great spider web a-tremble. The life that I touch for good or ill will touch another life, and that in turn another, until who knows where the trembling stops or in what far place and time my touch will be felt. Our lives are linked together. No man is an island.

But there is another truth, the sister of this one, and it is that every man is an island. It is a truth that often the tolling of a silence reveals even more vividly than the tolling of a bell. We sit in silence with one another, each of us more or less reluctant to speak, for fear that if he does, he may sound like a fool. And beneath that there is of course the deeper fear, which is really a fear of the self rather than of the other, that maybe the truth of it is that indeed he is a fool. The fear that the self that he reveals by speaking may be a self that the others will reject just as in a way he has himself rejected it. So either we do not speak, or we speak not to reveal who we are but to conceal who we are, because words can be used either way of course. Instead of showing ourselves as we truly are, we show ourselves as we believe others want us to be. We wear masks, and with practice we do it better and better, and they serve us well—except that it gets very lonely inside the mask, because inside the mask that each of us wears there is a person who both longs to be known and fears to be known. In this sense every man is an island separated from every other man by fathoms of distrust and duplicity. Part of what it means to *be* is to be you and not me, between us the sea that we can never entirely cross even when we would. "My brethren are wholly estranged from me," Job cries out. "I have become an alien in their eyes."

The paradox is that part of what binds us closest together as human beings and makes it true that no man is an island is the knowledge that in another way every man is an island. Because to know this is to know that not only deep in you is there a self that longs above all to be known and accepted, but that there is also such a self in me, in everyone else the world over. So when we meet as strangers, when even friends look like strangers, it is good to remember that we need each other greatly you and I, more than much of the time we dare to imagine, more than most of the time we dare to admit.

Island calls to island across the silence, and once, in trust, the real words come, a bridge is built and love is done —not sentimental, emotional love, but love that is *pontifex*, bridge-builder. Love that speaks the holy and healing word which is: *God be with you, stranger who are no stranger. I wish you well.* The islands become an archipelago, a continent, become a kingdom whose name is the Kingdom of God.

FATHER and Lord,
Most near and most far, listen to our silence before thee as well as to our prayers, because often it is the silence that speaks better of our need. Speak thy joy into our silence. Breathe thy life into our less than life, not for our own sakes only but for the sake of those to whom, with thy life in us, we may ourselves bring life.

Much as we wish, not one of us can bring back yesterday or shape tomorrow. Only today is ours, and it will not be ours for long, and once it is gone it will never in all time be ours again. Thou only knowest what it holds in store for us, yet even we know something of what it will hold. The chance to speak the truth, to show mercy, to ease another's burden. The chance to resist evil, to remember all the good times and the good people of our past, to be brave, to be strong, to be glad. We know that today as every day our lives will be touched by thee and that one way or another thou wilt speak to us before we sleep, for the very moments themselves of our lives are thy words to us. Give us ears to hear thee speak. Give us hearts to quicken as thou drawest near.   *Amen.*

6

Come and See

The people who walked in darkness
    have seen a great light;
those who dwelt in a land of deep darkness,
    on them has light shined.
Thou hast multiplied the nation,
    thou hast increased its joy;
they rejoice before thee
    as with joy at the harvest,
    as men rejoice when they divide the spoil.
For the yoke of his burden,
    and the staff for his shoulder,
    the rod of his oppressor,
    thou has broken as on the day of Midian.
For every boot of the tramping warrior in battle tumult
    and every garment rolled in blood
    will be burned as fuel for the fire.
For to us a child is born,
    to us a son is given;
and the government will be upon his shoulder,
    and his name will be called
"Wonderful Counselor, Mighty God,
    Everlasting Father, Prince of Peace."

ISAIAH 9:2–6

In one respect if in no other this metaphor of Isaiah's is a very relevant one for us and our age because we are also, God knows, a people who walk in darkness. There seems little need to explain. If darkness is meant to suggest a world where nobody can see very well—either themselves, or each other, or where they are heading, or even where they are standing at the moment; if darkness is meant to convey a sense of uncertainty, of being lost, of being afraid; if darkness suggests conflict, conflict between races, between nations, between individuals each pretty much out for himself when you come right down to it; then we live in a world that knows much about darkness. Darkness is what our newspapers are about. Darkness is what most of our best contemporary literature is about. Darkness fills the skies over our own cities no less than over the cities of our enemies. And in our single lives, we know much about darkness too. If we are people who pray, darkness is apt to be a lot of what our prayers are about. If we are people who do not pray, it is apt to be darkness in one form or another that has stopped our mouths.

But the prophecy of Isaiah is that into this darkness a great light will shine, and of course the proclamation of the Gospel, especially the wild and joy-drunk proclamation of Christmas, is that into this darkness there has already shone a light to dazzle the world with its glory and its terror, for if there is a terror about darkness because we cannot see, there is also a terror about light because we can see. There is a terror about light because much of what we see in the light about ourselves and our world we would rather not see, would rather not have be seen. The first thing that the angel said to the shepherds was, "Be not afraid," and he said it with the glory of the Lord shining round about them there in the fields because there was terror as well as splendor in the light of the glory of the Lord.

In the darkness of a church, the candles burn. They hold the darkness back, just barely hold it back. In the darkness of that Judean night, in the midst of nowhere, to parents who were nobody, the child was born, and whoever it was that delivered him slapped his bare backside to start the breath going, and he cried out, as each one of us cried out, at the shock and strangeness of being born into the darkness of the world. Then, as the Gospels picture it, all heaven broke loose.

The darkness was shattered like glass, and the glory flooded through with the light of a thousand suns. A new star blazed forth where there had never been a star before, and the air was filled with the bright wings of angels, the night sky came alive with the glittering armies of God, and a great hymn of victory rose up from them—Glory to God in the highest—and strange kings arrived out of the East to lay kingly gifts at the feet of this even stranger and more kingly child. This is how, after all the weary centuries of waiting, the light is said finally to have come into the world, as Luke proclaims it and Matthew, and they proclaim it of course in the language of faith and from the standpoint of faith.

But there is also the standpoint of history and the blunt language of fact. We live in a skeptical age where the assumption that most of us go by, consciously or otherwise, is that nothing is entirely real that cannot somehow be verified by science. It seems to me at best a dubious assumption, but it is part of the air that we breathe, so let us be as skeptical as our age about this story of Christmas. Let us assume that if we had been there that night when he was born, we would have seen nothing untoward at all. Let us assume that the darkness would have looked very much like any darkness. Maybe there were a few stars, the same old stars, or the moon. For a long time the only sound perhaps was the rough, rapid breathing of the woman in labor. If the tradition of the manger is accurate, there was the smell of hay, the great moist eyes of the cattle. The father was there, possibly a shepherd or two attracted by the light, if there was any light. There was a last cry of pain from the mother as the child was born, and then the cry of the child. In the distance maybe the lonely barking of a dog. The mother stares up at the rafters from where she is lying, too exhausted even to think of the child. Someone has taken him from her to wrap him up against the cold and darkness of the world. Maybe a mouse burrows deeper into the straw.

Maybe that is all we would have seen if we had been there because maybe that or something like that was all that really happened. In the letters of St. Paul, which are the earliest New Testament writings, there is no suggestion that the birth of Jesus was accompanied by any miracle, and in the Gospel of Mark, which is probably the earliest of the four, the birth plays no part. So a great many biblical scholars would agree with the skeptics that the great nativity stories of Luke and Matthew are simply the legendary accretions, the poetry, of a later generation, and that were we to have been present, we would have seen a birth no more or less marvelous than any other birth.

But if that is the case, what do we do with the legends of

the wise men and the star, the shepherds and the angels and
the great hymn of joy that the angels sang? Do we dismiss
them as fairy tales, the subject for pageants to sentimentalize
over once a year come Christmas, the lovely dream that never
came true? Only if we are fools do we do that, although
there are many in our age who have done it and there are
moments of darkness when each one of us is tempted to do it.
A lovely dream. That is all.

Who knows what the facts of Jesus' birth actually were?
As for myself, the longer I live, the more inclined I am to
believe in miracle, the more I suspect that if we had been
there at the birth, we might well have seen and heard things
that would be hard to reconcile with modern science. But of
course that is not the point, because the Gospel writers are
not really interested primarily in the facts of the birth but
in the significance, the meaning for them of that birth just
as the people who love us are not really interested primarily
in the facts of our births but in what it meant to them when
we were born and how for them the world was never the
same again, how their whole lives were charged with new significance. Whether there were ten million angels there or just
the woman herself and her husband, when that child was born
the whole course of history was changed. That is a fact as hard
and blunt as any fact. Art, music, literature, our culture itself,
our political institutions, our whole understanding of ourselves
and our world—it is impossible to conceive of how differently
world history would have developed if that child had not
been born. And in terms of faith, much more must be said
because for faith, the birth of the child into the darkness of
the world made possible not just a new way of understanding
life but a new way of living life.

Ever since the child was born, there have been people who have gotten drunk on him no less than a man can get drunk on hard liquor. Or if that metaphor seems crude, all the way down the twenty centuries since that child was born, there have been countless different kinds of people who in countless different kinds of ways have been filled with his spirit, who have been grasped by him, caught up into his life, who have found themselves in deep and private ways healed and transformed by their relationships with him, so much so that they simply have no choice but to go on proclaiming what the writers of the Gospels first proclaimed: that he was indeed the long expected one, the Christ, Wonderful Counselor, Mighty God, Everlasting Father, Prince of Peace—all these curious and forbidding terms that Christians keep on using in their attempt to express in language one thing and one thing only. That in this child, in the man he grew up to be, there is the power of God to bring light into our darkness, to make us whole, to give a new kind of life to anybody who turns toward him in faith, even to such as you and me.

This is what Matthew and Luke are trying to say in their stories about how he was born, and this is the truth that no language seemed too miraculous to them to convey. This is the only truth that matters, and the wise men, the shepherds, the star, are important only as ways of pointing to this truth. So what is left to us then is the greatest question of them all. How do we know whether or not this truth is true? How do we find out for ourselves whether in this child born so long ago there really is the power to give us a new kind of life in which both suffering and joy are immeasurably deepened, a new kind of life in which little by little we begin to be able to love even our friends, at moments maybe even our enemies, maybe at last even ourselves, even God?

Adeste fidelis. That is the only answer that I know for people who want to find out whether or not this is true. Come all ye faithful, and all ye who would like to be faithful if only you could, all ye who walk in darkness and hunger for light. Have faith enough, hope enough, despair enough, foolishness enough, at least to draw near to see for yourselves.

He says to ask and it will be given you, to seek and you will find. In other words, he says that if you pray for him, he will come to you, and as far as I know, there is only one way to find out whether that is true, and that is to try it. Pray for him and see if he comes, in ways that only you will recognize. He says to follow him, to walk as he did into the world's darkness, to throw yourself away as he threw himself away for love of the dark world. And he says that if you follow him, you will end up on some kind of cross but that beyond your cross and even on your cross you will also find your heart's desire, the peace that passes all understanding. And again, as far as I know there is only one way to find out whether that is true, and that is to try it. Follow him and see. And if the going gets too tough, you can always back out. Maybe you can always back out.

Adeste fidelis. Come and behold him, born the king of angels. Speak to him or be silent before him. In whatever way seems right to you and at whatever time, come to him with your empty hands. The great promise is that to come to him who was born at Bethlehem is to find coming to birth within ourselves something stronger and braver, gladder and kinder and holier, than ever we knew before or than ever we could have known without him.

D EAR God,
       In the darkness of the virgin's womb the holy child grows. In the darkness of the world's pain, the blessed light begins to kindle. In the darkness of our own doubting of thee and of ourselves, the great hope begins to rise again like a lump in the throat: the hope that thou wilt come to us truly, that the child will be born again in our midst, the Prince of Peace in a world at war, the hope that thou wilt ransom us and our world from the darkness that seeks to destroy us.

O Lord, the gift of new life, new light, can be a gift truly only if we open ourselves to receive it. So this is our prayer, Lord: that thou wilt open our eyes to see thy glory in the coming again of light each day, open our ears to hear the angels' hymn in the stirring within us of joy at the coming of the child, open our hearts to the transforming power of thy love as it comes to us through the love of all those who hold us most dear and have sacrificed most for us.

Be born among us that we may ourselves be born. Be born within us that by words and deeds of love we may bear the tidings of thy birth to a world that dies for lack of love. We ask it in the child's name. *Amen.*

part II

THE SOUGHT

For it is the God who said, "Let light shine out of darkness," who has shone in our hearts to give the light of the knowledge of the glory of God in the face of Christ.

2 CORINTHIANS 4:6

7

The Sign by
the Highway

Two others also, who were criminals, were led away to
be put to death with him. And when they came to the place
which is called The Skull, there they crucified him, and the
criminals, one on the right and one on the left. And Jesus
said, "Father, forgive them, for they know not what they
do." And they cast lots to divide his garments. And the people stood by, watching; but the rulers scoffed at him, saying,
"He saved others; let him save himself, if he is the Christ of
God, his Chosen One!" The soldiers also mocked him, coming up and offering him vinegar, and saying, "If you are the
King of the Jews, save yourself!" There was also an inscrip-
tion over him, "This is the King of the Jews."

One of the criminals who were hanged railed at him,
saying, "Are you not the Christ? Save yourself and us!" But
the other rebuked him, saying, "Do you not fear God, since
you are under the same sentence of condemnation? And we
indeed justly; for we are receiving the due reward of our
deeds; but this man has done nothing wrong." And he said,
"Jesus, remember me when you come in your kingly power."
And he said to him, "Truly, I say to you, today you will be
with me in Paradise." LUKE 23:32–43

A man drives along the highway in his car or a bus, or alongside the highway in a train, and he sees this and that: the signs and billboards—BURMA SHAVE, CHILDREN GO SLOW, PRINCE OF PIZZA. He sees the wash hanging out back, the reflection in the window of his own face whipped by the telephone poles that rush by or the dusty trees. And then maybe once in a while he looks up at the side of a cliff so high that he does not know how anybody ever got up there to do it, or at the concrete abutment of a bridge, and he sees written out in large, clumsy letters, usually done in white paint that has trickled down from the bottoms of the letters as though they were falling apart or melting, the message JESUS SAVES—just that, JESUS SAVES—with all the other signs going on with whatever they are saying, too. And if that man is like most of the people I know, including myself much of the time and in many ways, he will wince at the message; and that is really a very strange and interesting thing, both the message and the wincing.

God only knows what kind of a person must have crawled up there with his bucket and brush to slap the words on: a man or a woman, young or old, drunk or sober, by daylight or dark. And God only knows what reason he may have had for doing it, just that way, just there. But in our strange times, among people more or less like us, the effect at least of the words is clear enough: *Jesus Saves.* The effect more or less is that we do wince. And one way or another, I believe, we wince because we are embarrassed, and embarrassed for all kinds of reasons.

Embarrassed because the words remind us of old-time

religion and the sawdust trail and pulpit-pounding, corn-belt parsons, of evangelism in the sense of emotionalism and fundamentalism. We wince because there is something in the name "Jesus" itself that embarrasses us when it stands naked and alone like that, just *Jesus* with no title to soften the blow. It seems to me that the words "Christ saves" would not bother us half so much because they have a kind of objective, theological ring to them, whereas "Jesus" saves seems cringingly, painfully personal—somebody named Jesus, of all names, saving somebody named whatever your name happens to be. It is something very personal written up in a place that is very public, like the names of lovers carved into the back of a park bench or on an outhouse wall.

Maybe *Jesus Saves* written up there on the cliff or the abutment of the bridge is embarrassing because in one way or another religion in general has become embarrassing: embarrassing to the unreligious man because, although he does not have it any more, he has never really rooted it out of his soul either, and it still festers there as a kind of reproach; embarrassing to the religious man because, although in one form or another he still does have it, it seldom looks more threadbare or beside the point than when you set it against very much the same kind of seventy-five-mile-per-hour, neon-lit, cluttered and clamorous world that is represented by the highway that the sign itself looks down upon there. And maybe at a deeper level still, *Jesus Saves* is embarrassing because if you can hear it at all through your wincing, if any part at all of what it is trying to mean gets through, what it says to everybody who passes by and most importantly and unforgivably of all, of course, what it says to you is that you *need* to be saved. Rich man, poor man; young man, old man; educated and uneducated; religious and unreligious—the word is in its way an offense to all of them, all of us, because what it says in effect to all of us is, "You have no peace inside your skin. You are not happy, not whole." That is an unpardonable thing to say to a man whether it is true or false but especially if it is true because there he is, trying so hard to be happy, all of us are, to find some kind of inner peace and all in all maybe not making too bad a job of it considering the odds, so that what could be worse psychologically, humanly, than to say to him what amounts to "You will never make it. You have not and you will not, at least not without help." And what could be more presumptuous, more absurd, more pathetic, than for some poor fool with a cut-rate brush and a bucket of white paint to claim that the one to give that help is Jesus. If he said God, at least that would be an idea, and if you reject it, it is only an idea that you are rejecting on some kind of intellectual grounds. But by saying "Jesus" he puts it on a level where what you accept or reject is not an idea at all but a person; where what you accept or reject, however dim and far away and disfigured by time, is still just barely recognizable as a human face. Because behind the poor fool with his bucket there always stands of course the Prince of Fools himself, blessed be he, in his own way more persumptuous, more absurd and pathetic than anyone has ever managed to be since.

Jesus Saves. . . . And the bad thief, the one who according to tradition was strung up on his left, managed to choke out the words that in one form or another men have been choking out ever since whenever they have found themselves crossed up by the world: "Are you the Christ? Then save yourself and us." With the accent on the "us." If you are saviour, whatever that means, then why don't you save us, whatever that involves, save us from whatever it is that crosses us all up before we're done, from the world without and the world within that crosses us all out. Save us from and for and in the midst of the seventy-five-mile-per-hour, neon-lit criss-cross of roads that we all travel in this world. And then the good thief, the one on his right, rebuked the bad one for what he had said angrily, and then in effect said it again himself, only not angrily, God knows not angrily—said, "Jesus, remember me when you come in your kingly power." And finally the words of Jesus' answer, "Truly, I say to you, today you will be with me in Paradise," which are words no less crude than the ones trickling down the cliffside, in their way no less presumptuous, absurd, pathetic; words that express no theological idea as an idea, but words that it took a mouth of flesh to say and an ear of flesh to hear. I can imagine that the guards who had been posted there to see that the execution was carried out properly might themselves have felt something like embarrassment and turned away from the sheer lunacy of the scene.

Such a one as that save me? That one—spindle-shanked and crackpot who thinks he is God's son, bloodshot and drunk with his own torture, no less crossed up, crossed out than any other mother's son. Such a one as that—*Jesus*, scrawled up there on the concrete among the four-letter words and the names of lovers? Only somehow then, little by little, a deeper secret of the embarrassment begins to show through: not, can such a one as *that* save me, but, can such a one as that save *me?* Because I suspect that at its heart the painful wincing is directed less to the preposterousness of the claim that Jesus saves than it is directed to the preposterousness of the claim that people like ourselves are savable—not that we are such sinners that we do not deserve saving, but that we are so much ourselves, so hopelessly who we are—no better, no worse—that we wonder if it is possible for us to be saved. I suspect that the reason why the name "Jesus" embarrasses us when it stands naked is that it inevitably if only half consciously recalls to us our own names, our own nakedness. Jesus saves . . . whom? Saves Joe, saves Charlie, Ellen, saves me, saves you—just the names without any Mr. or Mrs., without any degrees or titles or social security numbers; just who we are, no more, no less. I suspect that it is at our own nakedness that we finally wince. And I suspect also that we know that in one sense anyway the words are right—right at least that, Jesus or no Jesus, something of great importance in our lives is missing, the one piece that all the other pieces have got to fit into if the entire picture of who we are is going to come together and be whole. Something whose name we do not know is missing, in the same way that sometimes in a room with friends we have the unaccountable feeling that some person is missing, someone who is supposed to be there and whom we need and want to be there even though we cannot think who it is and know him only by his absence.

The message on the cliffside calls us by name, and it is at our own names that I believe we wince most painfully because we know that we are less than our names: we are our names minus whatever belongs in the empty place. And the question a man is apt to ask in the darkest moments of his life is what salvation can there be, from anywhere, for the man who is less than his name.

A friend of mine had a dream that I think was a dream about this question. He dreamed that he was standing in an open place out under the sky, and there was a woman also standing there dressed in some coarse material like burlap. He could not see her face distinctly, but the impression that he had was that she was beautiful, and he went up to her and asked her a question. This friend of mine described himself to me once as a believing unbeliever, and the question that he asked her was the same one that Pontius Pilate asked Jesus, only he did not ask it the way you can imagine Pilate did—urbanely, with his eyes narrowed—but instead he asked it with great urgency as if his life depended on the answer, as perhaps it did. He went up to the woman in his dream and asked, "What is the truth?" Then he reached out for her hand, and she took it. Only instead of a hand, she had the claw of a bird, and as she answered his question, she grasped his hand so tightly in that claw that the pain was almost unendurable and prevented him from hearing her answer. So again he asked her, "What is the truth?" and again she pressed his hand, and again the pain drowned out her words. And then once more, a third time, and once more the terrible pain and behind it the answer that he could not hear. And the dream ended. What is the truth for the man who believes and cannot believe that there is a truth beyond all truths, to know which is to be himself made whole and true?

A child on Christmas Eve or on the day before his birthday lives for the presents that he will open the next day, and in this sense we all live like children. There are so many presents still to be opened—tomorrow, next month, next year —and in a way it is our looking forward to the presents that keeps us going. The unexpected friendship, the new job, seeing our names in the paper, falling in love, the birth of a child—all of these are presents that life gives if we want them badly enough and if we are lucky enough, and in a way every new day is a present to be opened just as today was and tomorrow will be. The old saying is that where there is life, there is hope, and I think that the hope that there is, is the hope that if not tomorrow or the next day, then some fine day, somehow, life will finally give us the present which, when we open it, will turn out to be the one that we have waited for so long, which is the one that will fill the empty place, which is the peace that passeth all understanding, which is the truth, salvation, whatever we want to call it. But one by one, as we open the presents, no matter how rich and wondrous they are, we discover that no one of them by itself, nor even all of them taken together, is the one of our deepest desiring—that ultimately, although her face is beautiful and draws us to her, life by herself does not have that final present to give. And to know that is the pain of it as again and again we reach out our hands to life for what we need most deeply, only to have it seized in the terrible grasp. My friend in his dream asked, "What is the truth?" and it might have seemed that the answer was the pain itself; that the ultimate truth is the pain of discovering that there is no ultimate truth. Except that beyond the pain was the answer that, because of the pain, he could not hear.

What is the truth? Take my hand. The truth is not in my hand. It is not mine to give, is not life's to give. What is the truth? It is not the answer to any question that we know how to ask. Can there be a truth that saves, can there be salvation, for those who have learned of life not to believe in salvation? Only on the other side of pain, the dream said. On the other side of the pained embarrassment at the words *Jesus saves*, which at its heart is a pained embarrassment at our own nakedness and incompleteness. On the other side of the bird-claw pain that brought tears to the eyes of the dreamer, which is the pain of hope betrayed. On the other side of the pain of the good thief, which is the pain of surrender, the pain of acknowledging finally our utter helplessness to save ourselves. In the depths of his own pain the good thief said, "Jesus, remember me when you come in your kingly power." Remember me. Remember me.

Jesus said, "I will." He said, preposterously, "Today you will be with me in Paradise." Spindle-shanked and crackpot, Mary's boy, God's son, flattened out on the face of a cliff, like a spider he scrambles up past the four-letter words and the names of lovers to slap up his preposterous pitch—*Jesus Saves*—and the preposterousness, the vulgarity almost, of those words that make us wince is finally, of course, the vulgarity of God himself. The vulgarity of a God who adorns the sky at sunrise and sundown with colors no decent painter would dream of placing together on a single canvas, the vulgarity of a God who created a world full of hybrids like us— half ape, half human—and who keeps breaking back into the muck of this world. The vulgarity of a God who was born into a cave among hicks and the steaming dung of beasts only to grow up and die on a cross between crooks. The vulgarity of a God who tampers with the lives of crooks, of clowns like me to the point where we come among crooks and clowns like you with white paint and a brush of our own and nothing more profound to say, nothing more precious and crucial to say finally, than just Yes, it is true. He does save—Jesus. He gives life, he makes whole, and if you choose to be, you will be with him in Paradise.

If it is not true, then all our religion or lack of it is only futility, busy-ness. If it is true, then it is we who are the crack-pots, the preposterous of the earth, if we do not draw near to him who saves. How? I do not know, except that through wanting to draw near, we have already drawn nearer. Through the moments of our own lives when something of his truth, his life, breaks through as it does in the sign by the highway and our wincing at it, as it breaks through in the sight of our own lonely and searching and most unsaved faces when we see them reflected in the train window whipped by the telegraph poles, as it breaks through in the occasional dream that is a holy dream. Moments like these.

How do we draw near? Through the prayers not just that we pray in a church, God knows, but through the any-time, anywhere prayer that is *Remember me, even though I don't remember you,* that is *What is the truth?* which is also a prayer. We draw near to him by following him even on clumsy and reluctant feet and without knowing more than two cents' worth at first about what is involved in following him—into the seventy-five-mile-per-hour, neon-lit pain of our world.

And if he is the truth and the life, we will find it out soon enough for ourselves, you can be sure of that, if we want to find it out, if we are willing to draw near in whatever idiotic way we can, all our reservations and doubts notwith-standing, because little by little we find out then that to be where he is, to go where he goes, to see through eyes and work with hands like his, is to feel like ourselves at last, is to become fully ourselves at last and fully each other's at last, and to become finally more even than that: to become fully his at last.

ALMIGHTY and everlasting God,
Only speak to us that we may hear thee. Then
speak to us again and yet again so that when in our hearts we
answer thee by saying No, we may at least know well to
whom we say it, and what it costs us to say it, and what it costs
our brothers, and what it costs thee. And when at those moments that we can never foretell we say Yes to thee, forgive
our halfheartedness, accept us as we are, work thy miracle
within us, and of thy grace give us strength to follow wherever love may lead.

We bless thee for him who shows us the way and is the
way and who will be, we pray, at the end of all our ways.
Grant that even on stumbling feet we may follow him into
the terrible needs of the human heart. Remember us. Remember us. For thy mercy's sake. *Amen.*

The Killing of Time

I am the resurrection and the life; he who believes in me, though he die, yet shall he live, and whoever lives and believes in me shall never die.   JOHN 11:25-26

W e all suffer to some degree from deafness, are certainly at best hard of hearing. We find it very hard to hear what other people are saying to us, either hard in the sense of difficult or hard in the sense of painful and sometimes hard in both senses at once. Somebody comes up and makes a remark about the weather, let us say, and all that we are able to hear or all that we allow ourselves to hear is someone making a remark about the weather. "Looks as though we might get some rain" is all that gets through to us when what he is really saying, of course—and sometimes we know this and sometimes we do not—is maybe, "I'm lonely. Be my friend, for Christ's sake. Speak," or maybe, "I know you are lonely." And in our deafness, our only response is to say, "Well we could certainly use it," and then we indicate that we have plenty of our own work to get on with. The truth of it is that if you really listen to another person, whether on the surface he is talking about the weather or predicting the outcome of the World Series or even preaching a sermon, if you really listen, you begin to realize that what he is really talking about is himself. He is saying, "Love me" or maybe "Hate me" or "Pity me," but always he is saying one way or another, "Listen to me. Know me." Only most of the time people like you and me are deaf to this. We hear only the words. We hear only what is most comfortable to hear. But once in a while, by the grace of God more often than not, we hear scraps at least of what people are actually saying.

My wife and I were buying groceries one day, and I was on one side of the store and she was on the other, and over a shelf of breakfast cereal and cake mix I said, "Don't forget the cream," and she said, "All right, but don't you forget you're trying to lose weight," and I said, "Oh well, you only live once." And then it happened, this thing that broke for a moment through my deafness. The store was nearly empty so that the woman at the checkout counter had no trouble hearing us. It was a hot, muggy afternoon, and she had been working hard all day and looked flushed and hectic there behind her cash register and the racks of Life Savers and chewing gum and TV guides, and when I said, "Oh well, you only live once," she broke into the conversation, and what she said was, "Don't you think once is enough?" That was it.

It was a mild jest and I laughed mildly and so did the boy carrying up some empty cartons from the cellar, but it was also very much not a jest because I had a feeling that what by some rare chance I had happened to hear was a human being saying something like this: "People come and people go, most of them strangers. I'm sick of them, and I'm sick of myself too. One day's very much like another." What I thought I heard was a human being saying, "I'll live my life out to the last, and I expect to have good days as well as bad. But when the end comes, I won't complain. One life will do me very nicely." Then somebody plunked a bottle of something down on the counter and the cash register rang open and the checkout clerk with her hair damp on her forehead said, "Don't you think once is enough?" Jesus said, "I am the resurrection and the life; he who believes in me, though he die, yet shall he live." It was life and death that she was talking about too, her own life and her own death, and by some fluke I happened to hear her despite that hardness of hearing that we all share. Even the Lord Jesus Christ somehow made himself heard that steamy August day among the detergents and floor waxes. "Whoever lives and believes in me shall never die." "Don't you think once is enough?" the woman said.

There are so many things to say, of course. One thing is that whether one life is enough or not enough, one life is all we get, at least only one life *here*, only one life in this gorgeous and hair-raising world, only one life with the range of possibilities for doing and being that are open to us now. William Hazlitt wrote that no young man believes that he will ever die, and the truth of the matter, I think, is that in some measure that is true of all men. Intellectually we all know that we will die, but we do not really know it in the sense that the knowledge becomes part of us. We do not really know it in the sense of living as though it were true. On the contrary, we tend to live as though our lives would go on forever. We spend our lives like drunken sailors.

The drive from one place to another place, for instance— an hour, two hours, whatever it is. You think of it as a kind of necessary evil that you have to endure in order to get wherever you are going, and you turn on the radio if you are driving, or if you are not driving maybe you take a nap or read the billboards, to "kill time," as the saying goes. And what a grim saying that is if you stop to think about it, because the time that you are killing, of course, is your own time, and there is precious little of it at that. One life on this earth is all that we get, whether it is enough or not enough, and the obvious conclusion would seem to be that at the very least we are fools if we do not live it as fully and bravely and beautifully as we can. Yet I do not believe that the woman at the checkout counter was any rarity. The world is full of people who in one way or another are by and large merely "getting through" their lives, who are killing their time, who are living so much on the surface of things and are so bad at hearing each other and seeing each other that it is little wonder that one life seems enough to them or more than enough: seeing so little in this world, they think that there is little to see and that they have seen most of it already so that the rest probably is not worth seeing anyway and there is nothing new under the sun. There are lots of people who get into the habit of thinking of their time as not so much an end in itself, a time to be lived and loved and filled full for its own sake, but more as just a kind of way-station on the road to somewhere else, to a better job or the next vacation or whatever, and all the interim time that remains to be killed starts looming up like a great mountain that has to be climbed, so that if there were a little button somewhere that we could push to make it disappear all at once, I am not sure how many of us would have the strength not to push it.

But there is no such button and we all tend to look for other ways to make the years go fast, that terrible kind of phrase again. You often hear the advice that if you keep busy, it will be over before you know it, and the tragedy of it is that it is true. Life is busy. It comes at you like a great wave, and if you handle things right, you manage to keep your head above water and go tearing along with it, but if you are not careful, you get pulled under and rolled to the point where you no longer know who you are or where you are going. Life is a very busy affair, and in many ways that is a fine and proper thing, but there are other things about life that are also fine and proper.

Late one winter afternoon as I was walking to a class that I had to teach, I noticed the beginnings of what promised to be one of the great local sunsets. There was just the right kind of clouds and the sky was starting to burn and the bare trees were black as soot against it. When I got to the classroom, the lights were all on, of course, and the students were chattering, and I was just about to start things off when I thought of the sunset going on out there in the winter dusk, and on impulse, without warning, I snapped off the classroom lights. I am not sure that I ever had a happier impulse. The room faced west so as soon as it went dark, everything disappeared except what we could see through the windows, and there it was— the entire sky on fire by then, like the end of the world or the beginning of the world. You might think that somebody would have said something. Teachers do not usually plunge their students into that kind of darkness, and you might have expected a wisecrack or two or at least the creaking of chairs as people turned around to see if the old bird had finally lost his mind. But the astonishing thing was that the silence was as complete as you can get it in a room full of people, and we all sat there unmoving for as long as it took the extraordinary spectacle to fade slowly away.

For over twenty minutes nobody spoke a word. Nobody *did* anything. We just sat there in the near-dark and watched one day of our lives come to an end, and it is no immodesty to say that it was a great class because my only contribution was to snap off the lights and then hold my tongue. And I am not being sentimental about sunsets when I say that it was a great class because in a way the sunset was the least of it. What was great was the unbusy-ness of it. It was taking un-labeled, unallotted time just to look with maybe more than our eyes at what was wonderfully there to be looked at with-out any obligation to think any constructive thoughts about it or turn it to any useful purpose later, without any weapon at hand in the dark to kill the time it took. It was the sense too that we were not just ourselves individually looking out at the winter sky but that we were in some way also each other looking out at it. We were bound together there simply by the fact of our being human, by our splendid insignifi-cance in face of what was going on out there through the window, and by our curious significance in face of what was going on in there in that classroom. The way this world works, people are very apt to use the words they speak not so much as a way of revealing but, rather, as a way of con-cealing who they really are and what they really think, and that is why more than a few moments of silence with people we do not know well are apt to make us so tense and uneasy. Stripped of our verbal camouflage, we feel unarmed against the world and vulnerable, so we start babbling about any-thing just to keep the silence at bay. But if we can bear to let it be, silence, of course, can be communion at a very deep level indeed, and that half hour of silence was precisely that, and perhaps that was the greatest part of it all.

THE SOUGHT

I said, "You only live once," and the woman said, "Don't you think once is enough?" and in a way she was right. In our semideafness and semiblindness, in our killing of time, our boredom, our thirst for the dream of tomorrow and our neglect of the miracle of today, to the degree that this or something like this is our life, once is certainly enough. But in another way, a thousand lives do not seem enough, not when we are really alive, and I wonder if there is any particular confusion about when we are really alive. I suspect that the truth of it is simply that we are alive when, instead of killing time, we take time. When in the midst of tearing around in our busy-ness trying to do something, we stop once in a while and just let ourselves be something, be who we are. When by unclenching our fists, we give life a chance to do something with us. When we take the little piece of time that we have in this world and pay attention to what it is telling us, not just to what it is telling us about the beauty of the sun as it sets, God knows, but to what it is telling us about all the wildness and strangeness and pain of things, the tears of things, the *lachrimae rerum*, as well as the joy of things.

If the time that lies ahead looks like a great mountain that must be climbed, rest assured that is just what it is, and that is good. It is good to climb mountains, and the view from the top is good, and so is the climbing itself lots of the time. But there is more to our time than the mountains. There is our spirit, our intuition as well as our reason, the wisdom of the flesh as well as the wisdom of the mind. There are our dreams to listen to as well as our transistors and there are games to play as well as work to be done. There is our occasional gift for being silent, by ourselves and together. And unless all of these things are happening, we are less than alive.

We are really alive when we listen to each other, to the silences of each other as well as to the words and what lies behind the words. "Looks as though we might get some rain," somebody says. *Speak to me for Christ's sake. Know me.* "Don't you think once is enough?" *I'm bored and tired as hell, if there's such a thing as hell. A cup of cold water.* We are really alive when we are together as human beings, when by sunset or daybreak or by the fluorescence of a grocery store or the shabby twilight of a church the walls between us crumble a little.

What I try to avoid because the word has become so threadbare in our time is that we are really alive, of course, when we manage somehow to love—when we love the mystery and beauty and terror that loom vast just beneath the air we move through, when we begin to hear a voice not just in the setting sun but in the earthquake, in the silence, in the agonies of men as well as in their gladness. We are really alive when we love each other, when we look at each other and think, "Grace and peace be with you, brother and friend." When there is such life as this, once is not nearly enough.

Yet it is all that we get—with these chances to be truly alive, this kind of life to love with. Then there is death, the final deafness, the final blindness, the final separation from each other and from God which with part of ourselves we have always wanted. Unlike the great oriental religions, Christianity takes death very seriously, which is of course why it also takes life very seriously, why there is such urgency about living it right and living it now. In the New Testament there is no doctrine of endless rebirths on the great wheel of life, no doctrine of a soul which by its nature cannot die. On the contrary, by our nature we do die, as Christianity sees it, with our bodies and souls as inextricably one in death as they are in life.

But if death is the end in Christianity, it is not the final end; it is the end of an act only, not the end of the drama. Once before out of the abyss of the unborn, the uncreated, the not-yet, you and I who from all eternity had been nothing became something. Out of nonbeing we emerged into being. And what Jesus promises is resurrection, which means that once again this miracle will happen, and out of death will come another realm of life. Not because by our nature there is part of us that does not die, but because by God's nature he will not let even death separate us from him finally. Because he loves us. In love he made us and in love he will mend us. In love he will have us his true sons before he is through, and in order to do that, one life is not enough, God knows.

So back to the grocery store again and the tired lady behind the cash register. Back to each other again and to the mountains we have to climb this year and every year. Back to the time again that will kill us finally better than ever we can manage to kill it. Thomas, doubting Thomas, was the one of the Twelve who asked the question that must have been on all of their minds. "Lord, we do not know where you are going," he said. "How can we know the way?" And Jesus said, "I am the way and the truth and the life."

Well, and we none of us know much about where we are going really, not in the long run anyway, beyond the next mountain. We keep busy. We climb. We learn. We grow. Hopefully. But we are going, I believe, much, much further than at this point we can possibly see, and in everything we do or fail to do, much more is at stake, I believe, than we dream. In this life and in whatever life awaits us, he is the way; that is our faith. And the way he is, is the way of taking time enough to love our little piece of time without forgetting that we live also beyond time. It is the way of hearing the lives that touch against our lives. It is the way of keeping silence from time to time before the holy mystery of life in this strange world and before the power and grace that surround us in this strange world. It is the way of love.

ALMIGHTY God,
    Praise be to thee for the night, for the time we lie asleep in the darkness, unconscious and unthinking, as mute and innocent as animals, as trees, as the ancient earth itself. Praise be to thee for the gentle hours of the night when no self-will, no words, no cleverness, separate us from the mystery simply of being—a stone, a bird, a leaf, a man, all brothers in the stillness, all the work of thy hands, sustained by thee.

Praise be to thee for giving us back the world, for the miracle of waking, new again, into the newness of another day. Praise be to thee for our freedom as men not simply to be thy children but to choose to be. Praise be to thee for our waking minds through which we not only live but know we live and can marvel at thy gift to us of life, can offer our lives to thee to use as thou wilt.

Guide us, we pray, down the unknown corridor of this

day and every day. Lead us, each one, to the one door of all the many doors that thou wouldst have him open. Give us courage to speak there the word that thou wouldst have us speak of love and of healing. Give us ears to hear thee speak at every turning of the way—to listen, to listen, to hear, and to obey, even when the heart within us faints. Help us to live this day as though it were the first of all our days or the last of all our days. *Amen.*

9

The Two Loves

Behold, you are beautiful, my love,
    behold, you are beautiful!
Your eyes are doves
    behind your veil. . . .
Your lips are like a scarlet thread,
    and your mouth is lovely. . . .
You are all fair, my love;
    there is no flaw in you. . . .
You have ravished my heart, my sister, my bride,
    you have ravished my heart with a glance of your eyes,
    with one jewel of your necklace.
How sweet is your love, my sister, my bride!
    how much better is your love than wine, . . .
                                    SONG OF SOLOMON 4:1–10, PASSIM

This is my commandment, that you love one another as I
have loved you. Greater love has no man than this, that a
man lay down his life for his friends.   JOHN 15:12–13

In one way it would be hard to imagine two biblical passages more different from one another than these. The
first one is part of a poem where the poet uses very rich and

sensuous imagery to evoke the beauty of his young bride; the
second is a few of the words that Jesus spoke to his disciples
the last time they ate together when he tried to summarize for
them what he believed was the very essence of the life that
men were created to live. In one way, you could hardly imagine two passages at greater variance with each other, but in
another way, you could say that they are simply variations on
the same theme. The theme, of course, is love.

On the other hand, you might want to object to that and
say that they are really about two different kinds of love, and in
some measure you would be right. Because the Song of Solomon is very openly and unashamedly about the sexual love of
a man for a woman, whereas Jesus speaks about the love that
leads a man to lay down his life, if need be, for his friends. A
great many people have pointed out that it is a pity that in the
English language we have only one word to do for them both;
and in a way it is a pity because life is confusing enough as it
is, and it would certainly make for greater clarity if we dis-
tinguished between sacred love and profane love, or sexual
love and brotherly love, or, to use the Greek words, between
eros love and *agape* love. Yet I believe that there is a kind of
unconscious wisdom in our English use of only one word,
love, to describe them both because at their deepest level I
believe that they are more nearly one than they are two. I believe that they are both expressions of a single deep human
impulse. But to see how they are one, as I believe they are, it
is important first to see how they are two.

The ancient Hebrew poet of the Song of Solomon writes,
"How sweet is your love, my sister, my bride! How much
better is your love than wine," and that is as good an image

as any for this first kind of love which is sometimes known
by the Greek word *eros*. He is saying that he loves her because her love is sweet, which is to say that he desires her
because in her beauty he finds her desirable. He loves her because she brings to him a gladness, a joy, which without her
he cannot have. He loves her because he needs her. Because
the key to understanding *eros* love is the word "need." *Eros*
is born of need, and *eros* is directed to that which, or the one
who, satisfies that need; and therefore *eros* is not only sexual
love, although the word "erotic" has come to mean that, but
it is any love that reaches up for what in itself it is not and
has not. The movement of *eros* is always upward. *Eros* is the
love of what is beautiful, the love of what is true, the love of
what is good, the love of what is missing and necessary. It is
the love of a man for a woman, but it is also the love of a child
for its parents. It is the love of a man for his work through
which he expresses himself and finds himself. *Eros* is ultimately the upward-reaching, inexhaustibly yearning love of
a man for what is infinitely desirable, and in that sense for
God. If I were asked to produce a picture of *eros*, I would
choose a little engraving by William Blake which shows the
tiny figure of a man standing on the great, curved flank of the
earth's surface. It is night-time, and the man, with his arms
outstretched, has his foot on the first rung of a ladder which
reaches up toward the moon. Underneath, in block capitals,
are the words: I WANT! I WANT!

    Eros is the love of what is wanted, what is needed, and
on the level of sexual need, biblical faith affirms *eros* as good.
In the first of the two creation stories in Genesis, the great
refrain after each new day has been brought into being is

"God saw that it was good," and after the sixth day, when God creates male and female and says to them to be fruitful and multiply, the refrain becomes, "And behold, God saw everything that he had made, and behold, it was very good." In other words, as the Bible sees it, man is good in his sexual nature no less than in his spirit because, like the rest of creation, man in his totality is created by a creator who is himself good.

In the second creation story, this is said again but in a more complex way. After God has planted his garden in Eden and filled it with good things and placed man in the midst of it, he says, "It is not good that man should be alone," so then he creates woman, Eve, to be "a helper fit for him." Adam says, "This at last is bone of my bone and flesh of my flesh," and "they are both naked and are not ashamed." Thus the myth presents man and woman as created to be helpers of one another, to complement one another as human beings, and their sexual relationship, far from being a cause for guilt, is a good both in itself and as a means toward that good end.

It is primarily from the Greek tradition that we inherit the idea that man is essentially a spiritual creature, a soul, who is temporarily tied down to a body which, like an animal, must be held in check and its appetites curbed until finally at death it is destroyed and the soul set free at last. But in biblical thought, man does not *have* a body so much as he *is* a body. He is a body into which God has breathed the breath of life, his spirit, and therefore it is not in spite of his body that he does God's will and becomes what he was created to become but in and through his body, his sexuality included. It is undoubtedly true that the rabbis justified the inclusion of the Song of Solomon in the canon of the Old Testament by the argument that those wonderfully earthy love poems can be read also as symbolic of God's love for Israel; but the fact that they considered the earthiness an acceptable symbol further exemplifies the biblical position.

But the Bible does not conclude its view of sexual *eros* by simply pronouncing it good. As long as they remain in the garden of their innocence, Adam and Eve are not ashamed of their nakedness, because it is God's good gift and a means of expressing not only their own delight in each other but their responsibility to fulfill and complete each other as persons. But as the myth continues, the serpent appears and persuades them to eat of the fruit of the tree of the knowledge of good and evil, and then, of course, all is changed. "Then the eyes of both were opened," as the myth puts it, "and they knew that they were naked, and they sewed fig leaves together and made themselves aprons." What the myth seems to be saying is that once they destroy their relationship with God and decide to be gods unto themselves and to follow their own wills rather than his, their relationship with each other, including its sexual dimension, is also distorted. Sex, instead of remaining an expression of their joy in each other and of their mission to nurture and increase each other's humanness, becomes a way in which each can use and dominate the other for his own purpose. That, it would seem, is why they are suddenly ashamed and afraid.

So many people think of the Bible as primarily a source of moral truth, a book of arbitrary and hopelessly outmoded rules of what is right conduct and what is wrong conduct morally conceived. The Song of Solomon is seldom read in churches, largely, I suppose, because it too radically threatens this view. But surely the Bible is not first of all a book of moral truth. I would call it instead a book of truth about the way life is. These strange old Scriptures present life as having been ordered in a certain way, with certain laws as inextricably built into it as the law of gravity is built into the physical universe. When Jesus says that whoever would save his life will lose it and whoever loses his life will save it, surely he is not making a statement about how, morally speaking, life *ought* to be. Rather, he is making a statement about how life *is*. When John writes that he who does not love remains in death, he is not pronouncing an ethical judgment but a universal insight into what it means to be human. Behind all such words is the conviction that God has created life in such a way—or if you do not like the word "God," you could say simply that life has come about in such a way—that if a man lives in defiance of God's law—or again, if you don't like the word "God," you might say if he lives in defiance of the laws of human nature—then that man invites his own destruction as surely as the man who lives in defiance of the law of gravity invites it.

Not to love *is*, psychically, spiritually, to die. To live for yourself alone, hoarding your life for your own sake, is in almost every sense that matters to reduce your life to a life hardly worth the living, and thus to lose it. These are living truths of which morality, necessary as it is for keeping us from each other's throats, is the bare, dead bones.

In the realm of sexual behavior, morality has taken a real beating in our day, and it was high time that it did. The sexual ethic of our Puritan and Victorian forebears, rooted in the Greek idea of the good soul in the bad body, was a pretty cheerless business which tended to look on sexuality as a dark and dangerous beast to be kept in chains except within the context of marriage, and even there to be endured rather than enjoyed. It was repressive and unrealistic and hedged round with taboos, and in most ways, I believe, we are well rid of it. But the tragedy, of course, is that no new understanding of the deep human truths beneath the old morality has come to replace it. And the result is a kind of psychological and emotional chaos.

Most of the old restraints are gone or going. Such purely practical restraints as the fear of pregnancy and venereal disease have been all but eliminated by the ingenuity of modern science. Pornography is available to anybody who has the money to buy it at the newsstand. As much as you can generalize about such matters, in the realm of sexual behavior the word seems to be increasingly, "Anything goes," or, among the more responsible, "Anything goes as long as nobody gets hurt," the trouble with which is how can anybody know in advance, in any complex human relationship, sexual or otherwise, who *is* going to get hurt psychologically, emotionally, spiritually? Or the word is, "Anything goes as long as you love each other," the trouble with which is that love here is likely to mean a highly romanticized, sentimental sort of enterprise that comes and goes like the pink haze it is.

What makes this a tragic situation, I believe, is not so much that by one set of standards or another it is morally wrong, but that in terms of the way human life is, it just does not work very well. Our society is filled with people for whom the sexual relationship is one where body meets body but where person fails to meet person; where the immediate need for sexual gratification is satisfied but where the deeper need for companionship and understanding is left untouched. The result is that the relationship leads not to fulfillment but to a half-conscious sense of incompleteness, of inner loneliness, which is so much the sickness of our time. The desire to know another's nakedness is really the desire to know the other fully as a person. It is the desire to know and to be known, not just sexually but as a total human being. It is the desire for a relationship where each gives not just of his body but of his self, body and spirit both, for the other's gladness and strengthening and peace.

And that is when *eros*, the love born of need, is indeed "sweet and better than wine" and when biblical faith blesses it, because the need of *eros* is really the need to become fully human as we were made to be. That is why at the heart of it, I believe, *eros* love is the same as *agape* love, the love that Jesus means when he says, "Greater love has no man than this, that a man lay down his life for his friends." By such love as this, I not only give life to my friend but also find it for myself. *Agape* love works as great a miracle in the heart that gives it as in the heart to which it is given, and to become fully a person I need to sacrifice myself in love no less than my friend needs my sacrifice. In other words, *eros*, the love that seeks to find, and *agape*, the love that seeks to give, spring finally, I think, from the same deep impulse of the human heart, which is the impulse to be one with each other and within ourselves and ultimately with God.

L ORD,
    Catch us off guard today. Surprise us with some moment of beauty or pain so that for at least a moment we may be startled into seeing that you are with us here in all

your splendor, always and everywhere, barely hidden, beneath, beyond, within this life we breathe.

When we meet as men and women, help us also to see beneath the differences of sex to our common humanity, our common needs, so that we may love and serve each other fully. Open our hearts to the knowledge that beneath our hunger for one another lies a deeper hunger yet, a deeper emptiness which finally only you can fill. Open our hearts to the knowledge that we can be fully each other's only when we are fully yours. *Amen.*

10

The Wedding at Cana

On the third day there was a marriage at Cana in Galilee, and the mother of Jesus was there; Jesus also was invited to the marriage, with his disciples. When the wine failed, the mother of Jesus said to him, "They have no wine." And Jesus said to her, "O woman, what have you to do with me? My hour has not yet come." His mother said to the servants, "Do whatever he tells you." Now six stone jars were standing there, for the Jewish rites of purification, each holding twenty or thirty gallons. Jesus said to them, "Fill the jars with water." And they filled them up to the brim. He said to them, "Now draw some out, and take it to the steward of the feast." So they took it. When the steward of the feast tasted the water now become wine, and did not know where it came from (though the servants who had drawn the water knew), the steward of the feast called the bridegroom and said to him, "Every man serves the good wine first; and when men have drunk freely, then the poor wine; but you have kept the good wine until now." This, the first of his signs, Jesus did at Cana in Galilee, and manifested his glory; and his disciples believed in him.   JOHN 2:1–11

L ike so much of the Gospel of John, the story of the wedding at Cana has a curious luminousness about it, the quality almost of a dream where every gesture, every detail, suggests the presence of meaning beneath meaning, where people move with a kind of ritual stateliness, faces melting into other faces, voices speaking words of elusive but inexhaustible significance. It is on the third day that the wedding takes place, the third day that Jesus comes to change the water into wine, and in the way of dreams the number 3 calls up that other third day when just at daybreak, in another way and toward another end, Jesus came and changed despair into rejoicing. There are the six stone jars, and you wonder why six —some echo half-heard of the six days of creation perhaps, the six days that preceded the seventh and holiest day, God's day. And the cryptic words that Jesus speaks to his mother with their inexplicable sharpness, their foreshadowings of an hour beyond this hour in Cana of astonished gladness and feasting, of a final hour that was yet not final. But beyond the mystery of what it means, detail by detail, level beneath level, maybe the most important part of a dream is the part that stays with you when you wake up from it.

It can be a sense of revulsion at some hidden ugliness laid bare. It can be a kind of aching homesickness for some beauty that existed only in the dream. There are dreams which it is impossible to remember anything about at all except that they were good dreams and that we are somehow the better for having dreamed them. But taking this story in John as a dream, I think that what we carry from it most powerfully is simply a feeling for the joy of it—a wedding that almost flopped except that then this strange, stern guest came and worked a miracle and it turned out to be the best wedding of all. Certainly it is because of the joy of it that it is remembered in the marriage service.

But joy or no joy, people also cry at weddings. It is part

of the tradition. Women are said to cry especially, all dressed
up in their white gloves and their best hats with the tears running down, but I have known grown men to cry too and
sometimes even the minister forgets to worry about whether
his robe is straight and whether the best man has remembered
the ring and has to hold tight to his prayer book to keep down
the lump in his own throat. Sometimes the tears are good
tears, tears as a response to the mystery not only of human
love but of human finitude, the transience of things; but more
often than not, I suspect, the tears that are shed at weddings
are not to be taken too seriously because they are mainly sentimental tears, and although I suppose that they do little harm,
I would be surprised to hear that they ever did much good.
To be sentimental is to react not so much to something that is
happening as to your own reaction to something that is happening, so that when a person cries sentimentally, what he is
really crying at very often is the pathos of his own tears.
When we shed tears at a wedding, our tears are likely to have
a great deal less to do with the bride and groom than with all
the old dreams or regrets that the bride and groom have oc-
casioned in us. In our sentimentality, we think, "How wonderful that they are going to live happily ever after," or "How
terrible that they are never going to be so happy again," and
then we relate it all to our own happiness or our own lost
happiness and weep eloquently at ourselves. It is all innocent
enough, surely, except that it keeps us just one step further
than we already are, and God knows that is far enough, from
the reality of what is going on outside our own skins; and the
reality of what is going on outside our own skins is the reality
of other people with all their dreams and regrets, their happiness, the pathos not of ourselves for once but of them.

The reality of the bride and groom, which is also their joy, is of course that they love each other; but whereas sentimentality tends to stop right there and have a good cry, candor has to move on with eyes at least dry enough to see through. They love each other indeed, and in a grim world their love is a delight to behold, but love as a response of the heart to loveliness, love as primarily an emotion, is only part of what a Christian wedding celebrates, and beyond it are levels that sentimentality cannot see. Because the promises that are given are not just promises to love the other when the other is lovely and lovable, but to love the other for better or for worse, for richer or for poorer, in sickness and in health, and that means to love the other even at half-past three in the morning when the baby is crying and to love each other with a terrible cold in the head and when the bills have to be paid. The love that is affirmed at a wedding is not just a condition of the heart but an act of the will, and the promise that love makes is to will the other's good even at the expense sometimes of its own good—and that is quite a promise.

Whether the bride and groom are to live happily ever after or never to be so happy again depends entirely on how faithfully, by God's grace, they are able to keep that promise, just as the happiness of us all depends on how faithfully we also are able to keep such promises, and not just to a husband or a wife, because even selfless love when it is limited to that can become finally just another kind of self-centeredness with two selves in the center instead of one and all the more impregnable for that reason.

Dostoevski describes Alexei Karamazov falling asleep and dreaming about the wedding at Cana, and for him too it is a dream of indescribable joy, but when he wakes from it he does a curious thing. He throws himself down on the earth and embraces it. He kisses the earth and among tears that are in no way sentimental because they are turned not inward but outward he forgives the earth and begs its forgiveness and vows to love it forever. And that is the heart of it, after all, and matrimony is called holy because this brave and fateful promise of a man and a woman to love and honor and serve each other through thick and thin looks beyond itself to more fateful promises still and speaks mightily of what human life at its most human and its most alive and most holy must always be.

A dream is a compression of time where the dreamer can live through a whole constellation of events in no more time than it takes a curtain to rustle in the room where he sleeps. In dreams time does not flow on so much as it flows up, like water from a deep spring. And in this way every wedding is a dream, and every word that is spoken there means more than it says, and every gesture—the clasping of hands, the giving of rings—is rich with mystery. Part of the mystery is that Christ is there as he was in Cana once, and the joy of a wedding, and maybe even sometimes the tears, are a miracle that he works. But when the wedding feast was over, he set his face toward Jerusalem and started out for the hour that had not yet come but was to come soon enough, the hour when he too was to embrace the whole earth and water it with more than his tears.

And so it was also, we hope, with the bride and groom at Cana and with every bride and groom—that the love they bear one another and the joy they take in one another may help them grow in love for this whole troubled world where their final joy lies, and that the children we pray for them may open them to the knowledge that all men are their children even as we are their children and as they also are ours.

H OLY Lord God,
Thine is this fair world in all its splendor, but ours is the freedom to destroy thy world. Thine is the beginning and the end of all our lives, but ours are our lives themselves, to hoard in misery or to give away in joy. Thine is the kingdom and the power and the glory, but ours is the ear that is deaf, the tongue that is mute, the eye that is blind. Thine is the Christ, but ours is the cross he died upon.

Have mercy upon us. Have mercy upon all to whom we ourselves show little mercy—the unloving and the unbeautiful, the bitter and the lonely, the very slow, the very old.

Have mercy upon those who love and who in their love are beautiful, for they too are often forgotten by us, their joy itself a barrier between their lives and ours.

O Lord, in sorrow and in joy open thou our lives to one another that we may live. Open thou our lives to thee that even in dying we may never die. *Amen.*

11

The Monkey-God

As the Father has loved me, so have I loved you; abide in
my love. If you keep my commandments, you will abide in
my love, just as I have kept my Father's commandments and
abide in his love. These things I have spoken to you, that my
joy may be in you, and that your joy may be full.

JOHN 15:9–11

Somewhere in the vast collection of writings that have
grown up around Buddhist tradition there is a story about
a meeting that is supposed to have taken place one day between the Buddha himself and an odd little creature known
as the monkey-god. I am not sure who this monkey-god was
exactly, but the story itself tells you clearly enough all that
you need to know about him. After the fashion of monkeys,
he was apparently impudent, ingenious and rather ludicrous,
but above all he was very vain and very boastful. These quali-
ties become apparent as soon as he and the Buddha come
face to face, because the very first thing he tries to do is to
prove that he, the monkey-god, is just as powerful as the great
Buddha himself, if not indeed more so. In order to demon-
strate this he sets about performing a number of quite aston-

ishing tricks, the kind of trumpery that you might expect
from a monkey-god under the circumstances, and all the
while he is performing them, the Buddha sits there, polite and
inscrutable but giving no particular sign of being impressed.
So finally, when he is plainly at his wits' end, the monkey-
god plays his trump card, which consists of taking one enormous leap into the air and disappearing from sight completely.
He is gone for five minutes or five centuries—it makes little
difference—but eventually he comes back again and then just
stands around for a while obviously eager for the Buddha to
ask him where he has been. But the Buddha says nothing at
all. So the monkey-god tells him anyway, explains that he has
just come back from the outermost limits of the universe and
implies that this is a journey that even the Buddha might find
reason to admire. Then he stands around a while longer, this
time hoping that the Buddha will ask him what he saw there.

But again there is no sound except for the sound of his
own rather rapid breathing, and again he is forced to answer
the question that has not been asked. He explains in some detail how, when he reached the outermost limits of the universe,
he saw there five huge granite pillars which extended up and
up until the tops of them were lost in the clouds. And what
does the Buddha think of that, he asks, looking up into the
Buddha's great, silent face. And this time the Buddha does answer, but not in words. Instead of saying anything, the Buddha simply raises his hand and holds it up there before the
monkey-god's eyes. And as the monkey-god looks at it, his
attention is drawn to the Buddha's fingers, and as he gazes at
them, he sees them not as fingers but as five huge granite pillars
which extend up and up until the tops of them are lost in the
clouds.

THE SOUGHT

As a Christian preacher, what I envy the Buddha more than I can say is his silence, and I envy the Buddhist monks and teachers the way they emulate that silence. I envy them because when you come right down to it, of course, the kinds of things that you talk about in religion are always very difficult and usually quite impossible to put into words. This is most obviously true when you try to talk about God, because words after all were invented to deal with a world of space and time, whereas by definition God exists beyond such categories altogether. To try to talk about him in terms of time and space, which are the only terms we know, is like a man who has been blind from birth trying to talk about colors in terms of sound and touch, which are the only terms he knows. The best you can do in either case is to speak in the language of symbol and metaphor.

The blind man says perhaps that a sunrise is like the sound of trumpets in a great cathedral or like the way the damp grass feels to your bare feet in the summertime. We say of God that he is like a father or a king or that when he draws near to us it is the way a man feels when he is plowing a field and suddenly uncovers a rich treasure so that in his joy he goes and sells all that he has in order to buy that field. These are useful as suggestions of the reality that they point to, but needless to say they are not the reality itself. And this is why I so admire the Buddha, who simply holds up his hand, or the Buddhist teacher who, when someone asks him about the meaning of life, for instance, maybe laughs out loud, or throws a handful of feathers up into the air, or maybe just turns his back and walks away.

If the meaning of life is just a string of theological words, then who cares about it one way or another and what difference does it make and why bother to say the words at all, even if in some sense they are true? But if it is a reality, then words cannot contain it, you can know it only when you experience it, and if life in general has meaning, then every part of life also has meaning and you can experience it perfectly well by watching the feathers fall to the ground or seeing the teacher walk away in silence. To put it in other terms, suppose that a man falls in love and that a friend of his comes up to him and asks what it is like to fall in love. There would appear to be two courses open to him. The first would be to try to tell his friend, to describe all the symptoms, to show him a poem on the subject, perhaps to produce a photograph of the one he loves, and so forth, as the result of which the friend will have a fairly comprehensive account but very little real understanding if any. The second course would be not to try to tell his friend, and this could be done in an infinite number of ways, one of which would be to put his hands on his friend's shoulders and push him out the back door with the suggestion that if he travels far enough in the direction he has been pushed he may himself find someone to fall in love with, and then, and only then, will he know fully what it is like.

If I, as a preacher, were an unusually brave man, I would do something like this from the pulpit. First of all I would stop speaking, and then I would perform some action of the kind that the prophets of Israel used to perform, because, like Buddhist teachers, they also got tired of words from time to time and resorted to other more direct means of pointing to the reality, for them, of God's judgment or of God's love. Like Jeremiah, I might take a potter's flask and hold it high above my head and speak a few words like Jeremiah's, saying, "Hear the word of the Lord, O people of this mighty nation.

Because you have forsaken me and gone whoring after other gods like wealth and power, because you have grown fat on your plenty and have given too little thought to the downtrodden peoples of the earth whom I love, because injustice and inequality thrive in your cities, thus says the Lord of hosts: I will break this people and their cities as one breaks a potter's vessel so that it can never be mended." Then I would take this earthen flask and dash it to bits before my congregation as Jeremiah dashed his in the Valley of Benhinnom. Or like Hosea I would tell the story of a man who married a prostitute, of how she was unfaithful to him after their marriage, giving herself to many lovers, and of how at last he drove her out of his house in anger only to take her back again because he found that he loved her still. Then I would say, or perhaps I would not need to say, that we are the prostitute and that it is God's love for us that will not let us go for all our unfaithfulness. I have sometimes wondered if perhaps it was the writers of the Gospels themselves who put into Jesus' mouth by way of explanation the words, "Consider the lilies of the field, how they grow; they neither toil nor spin; yet I tell you, even Solomon in all his glory was not arrayed like one of these." I have wondered if perhaps Jesus himself, when the incident actually took place, merely pointed to the lilies and said nothing at all.

It is not that words are useless but that words are not enough, and all preachers must sometimes wish that they could somehow manage to hold forth the reality itself, without which all their words are only words. But they have no props as a rule—no earthen flask to shatter in pieces, no handful of feathers, no field of lilies—and we are all such helplessly verbal creatures that if they did have them, we would be as embarrassed to see them used as they would doubtless be to use them.

Yet there is something that a preacher, that any Christian, can hold forth. And it is the experience that Jesus speaks of in the passage from John, quoted at the beginning of this chapter, and which is so deep a part of the unutterable reality of the faith. "These things I have spoken to you," he said, "that my joy may be in you, and that your joy may be full." He might have said, and I suspect that we might have expected him to say, "These things I have spoken to you that my righteousness may be in you," or "my mercy" or "my glory," but although all of these are implied here, the word he uses is "joy," and joy is the experience that he points to as the outermost limit and goal of all that he came in God's name and with God's power to give.

There is not one of us whose life has not already been touched somewhere with joy, so that in order to make it real to us, to show it forth, it should be enough for Jesus simply to remind us of it, to make us remember the joyous moments of our own lives. Yet this is not easy because, ironically enough, these are likely to be precisely the moments that we do not associate with religion. We tend to think that joy is not only not properly religious but that it is even the opposite of religion. We tend to think that religion is sitting stiff and antiseptic and a little bored and that joy is laughter and freedom and reaching out our arms to embrace the whole wide and preposterous earth which is so beautiful that sometimes it nearly breaks our hearts. We need to be reminded that at its heart Christianity is joy and that laughter and freedom and the reaching out of arms are the essence of it. We need to be reminded too that joy is not the same as happiness. Happiness

is man-made—a happy home, a happy marriage, a happy relationship with our friends and within our jobs. We work for
these things, and if we are careful and wise and lucky, we can
usually achieve them. Happiness is one of the highest achieve-
ments of which we are capable, and when it is ours, we take
credit for it, and properly so. But we never take credit for our
moments of joy because we know that they are not man-made
and that we are never really responsible for them. They
come when they come. They are always sudden and quick
and unrepeatable. The unspeakable joy sometimes of just being alive. The miracle sometimes of being just who we are
with the blue sky and the green grass, the faces of our friends
and the waves of the ocean, being just what they are. The joy
of release, of being suddenly well when before we were sick,
of being forgiven when before we were ashamed and afraid,
of finding ourselves loved when we were lost and alone. The
joy of love, which is the joy of the flesh as well as the spirit.
But each of us can supply his own moments, so just two more
things. One is that joy is always all-encompassing; there is
nothing of us left over to hate with or to be afraid with, to
feel guilty with or to be selfish about. Joy is where the whole
being is pointed in one direction, and it is something that by
its nature a man never hoards but always wants to share. The
second thing is that joy is a mystery because it can happen
anywhere, anytime, even under the most unpromising circumstances, even in the midst of suffering, with tears in its eyes.
Even nailed to a tree.

What Jesus is saying is that men are made for joy and
that anyone who is truly joyous has a right to say that he is
doing God's will on this earth. Where you have known joy,
you have known him. We are the monkey-gods, of course—

monkeys in origin, the sons of God in destiny, outrageous and ludicrous, vain and boastful. And in answer to all our words about ourselves, about the meaning of life, about him, the God who made us holds up before our wondering eyes not just his hand, like the Buddha, but the figure of a man whose face is marred almost beyond human semblance but who says, "These things I have spoken to you, have done for you, have died for you, that my joy may be in you, and that your joy may be made full."

HEAVENLY Father,
Thy whole creation, sun, moon, and stars, and this blessed earth which thou hast made with thy hands in all its beauty, and every creature of this earth whom thou hast given life, all of them shout forth in joy and praise of thee, save only man whose mouth is stopped with words. Forgive us what we speak and what we know not how to speak. Forgive our world, we pray thee, thy world, which thou hast left us free to grieve and break. Make thyself known to all who are broken in spirit or in flesh, and that is all of us. Grant us thy peace, Lord, which the world can neither give nor take away, thy peace that exists only in the eye of the storm, the heart of the battle. Grant us finally the joy of the man on the cross. We ask it in his name.   *Amen.*

12

The Rider

For God so loved the world that he gave his only Son, that whoever believes in him should not perish but have eternal life.   JOHN 3:16

The Greek word *chronos* means "time" in a quantitative sense, chronological time, time that you can divide into minutes and years, time as duration. It is the sense that we mean when we say, "What time is it?" or "How much time do I have?" or "Time like an ever-flowing stream," in one of the hymns that we sing. But in Greek there is also the word *kairos*, which means "time" in a qualitative sense—not the kind that a clock measures but time that cannot be measured at all, time that is characterized by what happens in it. *Kairos* time is the kind that you mean when you say that "the time is ripe" to do something, "It's time to tell the truth," a truth-telling kind of time. Or "I had a good time"— the time had something about it that made me glad. The ancient poet who wrote the Book of Ecclesiastes was using time in a *kairos* sense when he wrote of a time to weep and a time to laugh, a time to keep silence and a time to speak.

We live our lives in both kinds of time at once, but during Holy Week especially we live in *kairos* time, because although in one way it is a week like any other week with one day moving into another chronologically until the week is gone, in another way the time of this week does not move at all, as though the ever-flowing stream of chronological time stops flowing, and the rippled, dancing, light-refracting surface grows so smooth and still that if your eyes are open, you begin to be able to see deep down into the water, deep down into time, and what you see there you cannot say is really either past or present but simply *is*, because in *kairos* time, past and present have a way of melting into each other and finally melting away.

The donkey's hooves raise little puffs of dust as it jogs along the sun-baked street. The rider sits with his bare feet tucked in tight under the soft, round underbelly of his beast. In a gesture of extravagance, one of the men who have gathered along the way to watch rushes forward and spreads his cloak out in the street in front of the animal, and this makes it shy and break suddenly into a trot. Taken off guard, the rider is jolted backwards at a crazy angle, and for a second it looks as though he will lose his balance and fall; but then with a fistful of shaggy mane, he pulls himself straight again. A woman lifts her naked child off her shoulders and sets him down by the roadside, where he squats and relieves himself into the dust as the donkey and his rider clip-clop by. Several of the onlookers are waving branches of myrtle and willow and sprays of palm leaf. The face of the rider is shiny with sweat. It is not a big crowd that has come to watch, just a small one. Many of them have no idea what the fuss is all about and could not care less. It is something to see, that is all.

It is this rider, of course, who gives the *kairos* time of

Holy Week its quality, its taste, its shape. It is his time, it is his week, and to live the week beneath the surface of eating, working, sleeping, is to live it close to him the way on the birthday or death day of somebody you love, you live that day close to him or, to turn it around, he lives that day in you.

On his last evening, they eat supper together for the last time, the rider and his friends, in some large room, upstairs somewhere in that city, a real room with things in it carpentered out of wood, coarse cloth, ragged moth at the candle flame, clink of pottery. Hands of bone and muscle move through the air, the sounds that men make eating. One of them wipes the back of his hand across his bearded mouth. Another eats like a drunk, never once taking his eyes off the one face of all their faces that is still, in the way the air just before a storm is still. As was the custom, the rider gets up to bless the bread, gives thanks for it; and as was the custom, he takes the loaf up into his hands and breaks it for them. Then the unaccustomed thing. He gives the loaf a name, his body, the dark wine a name, his blood, whatever he means by it, and tells them to eat and drink, although God knows they have no stomach for food now and their mouths are clumsy and spit-dry with, among other things, fear. In other words, he tells them to take his life into themselves and live it for him.

Ever since, the bread has been broken, the wine poured out, in commemoration of his death. Some come, not so many any more but always some, always enough, and the Lord knows why they do, why we do. Probably for the same reason that for century after century men have always come —because although there is much that we cannot understand, much that we cannot believe, the inexorable life in him draws us to him the way a glimmer of light draws a man who has lost his way in the dark. Because we are hungry for more than bread. Because we are thirsty for more than wine. That is the reason you have for coming to such a table, the reason I have for coming, and that is the only reason we need to have, thank God.

War is hell, but sometimes in the midst of that hell men do things that heaven itself must be proud of. A hand grenade is hurled into a group of men. One of the men throws himself on top of it, making his body a living shield. In the burst of wild fire he dies, and the others live. Heroism is only a word, often a phony one. This is an action for which there is no good word because we can hardly even imagine it, let alone give it its proper name. Very literally, one man takes death into his bowels, takes fire into his own sweet flesh, so that the other men can take life, some of them men he hardly knows.

Who knows why a man does such a thing or what thoughts pass through his mind just before he does it. Maybe no thoughts at all. Maybe if he stopped to think, he would never do it. Maybe he just acts spontaneously out of his passion the way, when you are a child and somebody attacks your brother, you attack the attacker with no fear for yourself but just because it is your brother and somebody is attacking him. Or if you are a cynic, you might say that a man must be temporarily insane to do such a thing because no man in his right mind would ever willingly give his life away, hardly even for somebody he loved, let alone for people he barely knows. Or that he must have acted out of a crazy thirst for glory, believing that not even death was too high a price to pay for a hero's honors. Or if you are an idealist, you might insist that although the human spirit is full of darkness, every once in a while it is capable of the Godlike act. Maybe in some complex way, something of all of these is involved. It is impossible for us to imagine the motive.

But I think that it is not so hard to imagine how the men whose lives are saved might react to the one who died to save them—not so hard, I suppose, for the obvious reason that most of us are more experienced at receiving sacrifices than at making them. In their minds' eyes, those saved men must always see the dead one where he lay in the ruins of his own mortality, and I suspect that at least part of what they feel must be a revulsion so strong that they come to believe that if they could somehow have stopped him from doing what he did, they would have stopped him. We say "life at any price," but I have the feeling that to have somebody else pay such a price for us would be almost more than we would choose to bear. I have the feeling that given the choice, we would not have let him do it, not for his sake but for our own sakes.

Because we have our pride, after all. We make our own way in the world, we fight our own battles, we are not looking for any handouts, we do not want something for nothing. It threatens our self-esteem, our self-reliance. And because to accept such a gift from another would be to bind us closer to him than we like to be bound to anybody. And maybe most of all because if another man dies so that I can live, it imposes a terrible burden on my life. From that point on, I cannot live any longer just for myself. I have got to live also somehow for him, as though in some sense he lives through me now as, in another sense, I live through him. If what he would have done with his life is going to be done, then I have got to do it. My debt to him is so great that the only way I can approach paying it is by living a life as brave and beautiful as his death. So maybe I would have prevented his dying if I could, but since it is too late for that, I can only live my life for what it truly is: not a life that is mine by natural right, to live any way I choose, but a life that is mine only because he gave it to me, and I have got to live it in a way that he also would have chosen.

He died twenty centuries ago, or dies this evening or will die tomorrow, and in his case there seems no mystery about the motive because as he understood it anyway, he died for us, died because, in some way that he did not try to explain, his death would make all the difference, for everybody, until the end of time. Does it? Does it?

It was so long ago. We do not even know what he looked like. (Or do we—would something in us recognize him if he were to appear before us?) Does that ancient death make any difference to people like us who live in a world that he could not possibly have imagined, a world of men, for many of whom God is dead? Is the death of Christ a death that really matters any more except in the dim way that any noble death might be said to matter?

All I can say is that I would not be writing these words unless I believed that the answer is Yes, that his death does make all the difference, even for us. I believe that by his dying he released into the world an entirely new kind of life, his kind of life, that has flowed down through the tragic centuries like water through a dry land, making alive and whole all who will only kneel to drink. And that is the only reason why it is not blasphemy to speak of the Friday of his unspeakable death as Good Friday.

Friday was the day of his crucifixion, the day of the last cry from the cross, which may have been "My God, my God, why have you forsaken me?" or may have been just the last wordless bellow of a man being tortured to death. Friday is the day when, for three hours, there is said to have been darkness over the face of the earth, the day of defeat and despair. And Sunday is just the opposite kind of day, because on Sunday it seemed that the death had not stuck, somehow the life had broken through again with all the power it had always had to heel and transform the lives it touched. Sunday is the day of rising sun, victory, great hope.

In between these two days there was Saturday, the day when nothing much happened at all. He was dead, and that was that. The two other days were given their own names as the centuries went by: Friday became Good Friday and Sunday became Easter. But Saturday has remained just plain Saturday or the Sabbath, as the Jews speak of it, the seventh day. The Gospels say almost nothing about it. The high priests and Pharisees got permission from the Roman procurator to post a guard at the tomb in case the disciples should try to steal the corpse. As for the disciples themselves, all we are told is that "on the sabbath they rested according to the commandment." You can imagine the kind of rest that it must have been—scared for their own skins, too stunned even for grief, all their dreams in ruins, and yet waiting, waiting, waiting for they probably were not sure what.

The Hungering Dark

O that thou wouldst rend the heavens and come down,
that the mountains might quake at thy presence—
as when fire kindles brushwood and the fire causes water
    to boil—
to make thy name known to thy adversaries,
and that the nations might tremble at thy presence! . . .
There is no one that calls upon thy name,
that bestirs himself to take hold of thee;
for thou hast hid thy face from us,
and hast delivered us into the hand of our iniquities.

ISAIAH 64: 1–2, 7

"And there will be signs in sun and moon and stars, and upon the earth distress of nations in perplexity at the roaring of the sea and the waves, men fainting with fear and with foreboding of what is coming on the world; for the powers of the heavens will be shaken. And then they will see the Son of man coming in a cloud with power and great glory. Now when these things begin to take place, look up and raise your heads, because your redemption is drawing near."

LUKE 21:25–28

About twenty years ago I was in Rome at Christmastime, and on Christmas Eve I went to St. Peter's to see the Pope celebrate mass. It happened also to be the end of Holy Year, and there were thousands of pilgrims from all over Europe who started arriving hours ahead of when the mass was supposed to begin so that they would be sure to find a good place to watch from, and it was not long before the whole enormous church was filled. I am sure that we did not look like a particularly religious crowd. We were milling around, thousands of us, elbowing each other out of the way to get as near as possible to the papal altar with its huge canopy of gilded bronze and to the aisle that was roped off for the Pope to come down. Some had brought food to sustain them through the long wait, and every once in a while singing would break out like brush fire—"Adeste Fidelis" and "Heilige Nacht" I remember especially because everybody seemed to know the Latin words to one and the German words to the other—and the singing would billow up into the great Michelangelo dome and then fade away until somebody somewhere started it up again. Whatever sense anybody might have had of its being a holy time and a holy place was swallowed up by the sheer spectacle of it—the countless voices and candles, and the marble faces of saints and apostles, and the hiss and shuffle of feet on the acres of mosaic.

Then finally, after several hours of waiting, there was suddenly a hush, and way off in the flickering distance I could see that the Swiss Guard had entered with the golden throne on their shoulders, and the crowds pressed in toward the aisle, and in a burst of cheering the procession began to work its slow way forward.

What I remember most clearly, of course, is the Pope himself, Pius XII as he was then. In all that Renaissance of splendor with the Swiss Guard in their scarlet and gold, the Pope himself was vested in plainest white with only a white skullcap on the back of his head. I can still see his face as he was carried by me on his throne—that lean, ascetic face, gray-skinned, with the high-bridged beak of a nose, his glasses glittering in the candlelight. And as he passed by me he was leaning slightly forward and peering into the crowd with extraordinary intensity.

Through the thick lenses of his glasses his eyes were larger than life, and he peered into my face and into all the faces around me and behind me with a look so keen and so charged that I could not escape the feeling that he must be looking for someone in particular. He was not a potentate nodding and smiling to acknowledge the enthusiasm of the multitudes. He was a man whose face seemed gray with waiting, whose eyes seemed huge and exhausted with searching, for someone, some *one*, who he thought might be there that night or any night, anywhere, but whom he had never found, and yet he kept looking. Face after face he searched for the face that he knew he would know—was it this one? was it this one? or this one?—and then he passed on out of my sight. It was a powerful moment for me, a moment that many other things have crystallized about since, and I felt that I knew whom he was looking for. I felt that anyone else who was really watching must also have known.

And the cry of Isaiah, "O that thou wouldst rend the heavens and come down, that the mountains would quake at thy presence . . . that the nations might tremble at thy presence! . . . There is no one that calls upon thy name, that bestirs himself to take hold of thee, for thou hast hid thy face from us, and hast delivered us into the hands of our iniquities."

In one sense, of course, the face was not hidden, and as the old Pope surely knew, the one he was looking for so hard was at that very moment crouched in some doorway against the night or leading home some raging Roman drunk or waiting for the mass to be over so he could come in with his pail and his mop to start cleaning up that holy mess. The old Pope surely knew that the one he was looking for was all around him there in St. Peter's. The face that he was looking for was visible, however dimly, in the faces of all of us who had come there that night mostly, perhaps, because it was the biggest show in Rome just then and did not cost a cent but also because we were looking for the same one he was looking for, even though, as Isaiah said, there were few of us with wit enough to call upon his name. The one we were looking for was there then as he is here now because he haunts the world, and as the years have gone by since that Christmas Eve, I think he has come to haunt us more and more until there is scarcely a place any longer where, recognized or unrecognized, his ghost has not been seen. It may well be a post-Christian age that we are living in, but I cannot think of an age that in its own way has looked with more wistfulness and fervor toward the ghost at least of Christ.

God knows we are a long way from the brotherhood of man, and any theory that little by little we are approaching the brotherhood of man has to reckon that it was out of the

Germany of Goethe and Brahms and Tillich that Dachau and Belsen came and that it is out of our own culture that the weapons of doom have come and the burning children. Yet more and more, I think, although we continue to destroy each other, we find it harder to hate each other.

Maybe it is because we have seen too much, literally *seen* too much, with all the ugliness and pain of our destroying flickering away on the blue screens across the land—the bombings and the riots, the nightmare in Dallas, the funeral in Atlanta. Maybe it is because having no cause holy enough to die for means also having no cause holy enough to hate for. But also I think that is because as men we have tried it so long our own grim way that maybe we are readier than we have ever been before to try it the way that is Christ's—whether we call upon his name or not.

Out there beyond this world there are more worlds and beyond them more worlds still, and maybe on none of them is there anything that we would call life, only barrenness, emptiness, silence. But here in this world there is life, we are life, and we begin to see, I think, that negatively, maybe nothing is worth the crippling and grieving of life. We begin to see that, positively, maybe everything glad and human and true and with any beauty in it depends on cherishing life, on breathing more life into this life that we are. However uncertainly and ambiguously, something at least in the world seems to be moving that way. I cannot believe that it is just fear of the bomb that has kept us as long as this from a third world war, or that it is just prudence and political pressure that slowly and painfully move the races and the nations to where they can at least begin to hear all the guilt and fear that have kept them apart for so long. I cannot believe that it is just a fad that young men in beards and sandals refuse in the name of love to bear arms or that it is entirely a joke that with Allen Ginsberg and Humphrey Bogart, Jesus of Nazareth is postered on undergraduate walls. Call it what you will, I believe that something is stirring in the hearts of men to which the very turbulence of our times bears witness. It is as if the moral and spiritual struggle that has always gone on privately in the consciences of the conscientious has exploded into the open with force enough to shake history itself no less than our private inner histories.

Maybe it will shake us to pieces, maybe it has come too late, but at least I believe that there are many in the world who have learned what I for one simply did not know twenty years ago in Rome: that wherever you look beneath another's face to his deepest needs to be known and healed, you have seen the Christ in him; that wherever you have looked to the deepest needs beneath your own face—among them the need to know and to heal—you have seen the Christ in yourself. And if this is what we have seen, then we have seen much, and if this is what the old Pope found as he was carried through the shadow and shimmer of his church, then he found much. Except that I have the feeling that he was looking for more, that in the teeming mystery of that place he was looking not just for the Christ in men but for the Christ himself, the one who promised that the son of man would come again in a cloud with power and great glory.

"There will be signs in sun and moon and stars," he said, "and upon the earth distress of nations in perplexity at the roaring of the sea and the waves, men fainting with fear and with foreboding," and then, at just such a time, we are tempted to say, as our own time, "look up and raise your

heads," he said, "because your redemption is drawing near."
And the words of Jesus are mild compared with the words of
a later generation. The Son of Man with face and hair as
white as snow and eyes of fire, the two-edged sword issuing
from his mouth. The last great battle with the armies of
heaven arrayed in white linen, and the beast thrown into the
lake of fire so that the judgment can take place and the
thousand years of peace. Then the heavenly city, New Jerusalem, coming down out of heaven like a bride adorned for
her husband, and the great voice saying, "Behold . . . ."
The New Testament ends, of course, with the words, "Come,
Lord Jesus," come again, come back and inaugurate these
mighty works, and I always remember a sign that I used to
pass by in Spanish-speaking East Harlem that said simply,
"Pronto viene, Jesus Cristo."

Surely there is no part of New Testament faith more
alien to our age than this doctrine of a second coming, this
dream of holiness returning in majesty to a world where for
centuries holiness has shone no brighter than in the lines of a
certain kind of suffering on faces like yours and mine. Partly,
I suppose, it is alien because of the grotesque, Hebraic images
it is clothed in. Partly too, I suppose, it is alien to us because
we have come to associate it so closely with the lunatic
fringe—the millennial sects climbing to the tops of hills in
their white robes to wait for the end of the world that never
comes, knocking at the backdoor to hand out their tracts
and ask if we have been washed in the blood of the lamb.

But beneath the language that they are written in and
the cranks that they have produced, if cranks they are, I
suspect that what our age finds most alien in these prophecies
of a second coming, a final judgment and redemption of the

world, is their passionate hopefulness. "Faith, hope, love," Paul wrote, "these three—and the greatest of these is love," and yes, love. We understand at last something about love. Even as nations we have come to understand at last something about love, at least as a practical necessity, a final expedient, if nothing else. We understand a little that if we do not feed the hungry and clothe the naked of the world, if as nations, as races, we do not join forces against war and disease and poverty in something that looks at least like love, then the world is doomed. God knows we are not very good at it, and we may still blow ourselves sky high before we are through, but at least maybe we have begun as a civilization to see what it is all about. And just because we have seen it, if only through a glass, darkly, just because maybe love is not so hard to sell the world as once it was, perhaps Paul would have written for us: "Love, yes, of course, love. But for you and your time, the greatest of these is hope because now it is hope that is hardest and rarest among men."

We have our hopes of course. This election year especially, jaded as you get after a while, the hope that out of all these faces that we come to know like the faces of importunate friends there will emerge a face to trust. The hope that if the lives of a Gandhi, a Martin Luther King, cannot transform our hearts, then maybe at least their deaths will break our hearts, break them enough to let a little of their humanity in. The hope that even if real peace does not come to the world, at least the worst of the killing will stop. The hope that as individuals, that you as you and me as me, will somehow win at least a stalemate against the inertias, the lusts, the muffled cruelties and deceits that we do battle with, all of us, all the time. The hope that by some chance today I will see a friend, that by some grace today I will be a friend. These familiar old hopes. No one of them is enough to get us out of bed in the morning but maybe together they are, must be, because we do get out of bed in the morning, we survive the night.

There is a Hebrew word for hope, *gāwāh*, whose root means to twist, to twine, and it is a word that seems to fit our brand of hoping well. The possibility that this good thing will happen and that that bad thing will not happen, a hundred little strands of hope that we twist together to make a cable of hope strong enough to pull ourselves along through our lives with. But we hope so much only for what it is reasonable to hope for out of the various human possibilities before us that even if we were to play a child's game and ask what do we hope for most in all the world, I suspect that our most extravagant answers would not be very extravagant. And this is the way of prudence certainly because to hope for more than the possible is to court despair. To hope for more than the possible is to risk becoming the ones who wait, helpless and irrelevant in their white robes, for a deliverance that never comes. To hope for more than the possible is a kind of madness.

For people like us, the reasonably thoughtful, reasonably reasonable and realistic people like us, this apocalyptic hope for the more than possible is too hopeful. We cannot hope such a fantastic hope any more, at least not quite, not often. It is dead for us, and we have tried to fill the empty place it left with smaller, saner hopes that the worst possibilities will never happen and that a few of the better possibilities may happen yet. And all these hopes twisted together do make hope enough to live by, hope enough to see a little way into the darkness by. But the empty place where the great hope used to be is mostly empty still, and the darkness hungers still for the great light that has gone out, the crazy dream of holiness coming down out of heaven like a bride adorned for us.

We cannot hope that hope any more because it is too fantastic for us, but maybe if in some dim, vestigial way we are Christians enough still to believe in mystery, maybe if beneath all our sad wisdom there is some little gibbering of madness left, then maybe we are called to be in some measure fantastic ourselves, to say at least maybe to the possibility of the impossible. When Jesus says that even as the world writhes in what may well be its final agony, we must raise our heads and look up because our redemption is near, maybe we are called upon to say not yes, because yes is too much for us, but to say maybe, maybe, because maybe is the most that hope can ever say. Maybe it will come, come again, come pronto. Pronto viene, Jesus Cristo.

Where do they come from, the Christ, the Buddhas? The villains we can always explain by the tragic conditions that produced them—the Hitlers, the Oswalds—but the births of the holy ones are in a way always miraculous births, and when they come, they move like strangers through the world. History does not produce holiness, I think. Saints do not evolve. If we cannot believe in God as a noun, maybe we can still believe in God as a verb. And the verb that God is, is transitive, it takes an object, and the object of the verb that God is, is the world. To love, to judge, to heal, to give Christs to. The world. The thousand thousand worlds.

Certainly a Christian must speak to the world in the language of the world. He must make the noblest causes of the world his causes and fight for justice and peace with the world's weapons—with Xerox machines and demonstrations and social action. He must reach out in something like love to what he can see of Christ in every man. But I think he must also be willing to be fantastic, or fantastic in other ways too, because at its heart religious faith is fantastic. Because Christ himself was fantastic with his hair every whichway and smelling of fish and looking probably a lot more like Groucho Marx than like Billy Budd as he stood there with his ugly death already thick as flies about him and said to raise our heads, raise our heads for Christ's sake, because our redemption is near.

Maybe holiness will come again. Maybe not as the Son of Man with eyes of fire and a two-edged sword in his mouth, but as a child who has maybe already been born into our world and beneath whose face the face of Christ is at this moment starting to burn through like the moon through clouds. Or if even that is too supernatural for us, maybe it will come in majesty from some other world because we have begun to take seriously the fantastic thought that maybe we are not alone in the universe.

Who knows what will happen? Except that in a world without God, in a way we do know. In a world without God we know at least that the thing that will happen will be a human thing, a thing no better and no worse than the most that humanity itself can be. But in a world with God, we can never know what will happen—maybe that is the most that the second coming can mean for our time—because the thing that happens then is God's thing, and that is to say a new and unimaginable and holy thing that humanity can guess at only in its wildest dreams. In a world with God, we come together in a church to celebrate, among other things, a mystery and to learn from, among other things, our ancient and discredited dreams.

It is madness to hope such a hope in our grim and sober times, madness to peer beyond the possibilities of history for the impossibilities of God. And there was madness among other things in the face of the old Pope that gaudy night with Hitler's Jews on his conscience maybe and whatever he died of already on its way to killing him. There was anxiety in his face, if I read it right, and weariness, and longing, longing. And to this extent his face was like your face and my face, and I would have had no cause to remember it so long. But there was also madness in that old man's face, I think. Like a monkey, his eyes were too big, too alive, too human for his face. And it is the madness that has haunted me through the years. Madness because I suspect that he hoped that Christ himself had come back that night as more than just the deepest humanness of every man's humanity, that Impossibility itself stood there resplendent in that impossible place.

He was not there, he had not come back, and as far as I know he has not come back yet. It is fantastic, of course, to think that he might, but that should not bother too much the likes of us. It is fantastic enough just that preachers should stand up in their black gowns making fools of themselves when they could be home reading the papers where only their children need know they are fools. It is fantastic that people should listen to them. It is fantastic that in a world like ours there should be something in us still that says at least maybe, maybe, to the fantastic possibility of God at all.

So in Christ's name, I commend this madness and this

fantastic hope that the future belongs to God no less than the past, that in some way we cannot imagine holiness will return to our world. I know of no time when the world has been riper for its return, when the dark has been hungrier. Thy kingdom come . . . we do shew forth the Lord's death till he come . . . and maybe the very madness of our hoping will give him the crazy, golden wings he needs to come on. I pray that he will come again and that you will make it your prayer. We need him, God knows.

"He who testifies to these things says, 'Surely I am coming soon.' Amen. Come, Lord Jesus."

L ORD Jesus Christ,
Help us not to fall in love with the night that covers us but through the darkness to watch for you as well as to work for you; to dream and hunger in the dark for the light of you. Help us to know that the madness of God is saner than men and that nothing that God has wrought in this world was ever possible.

Give us back the great hope again that the future is yours, that not even the world can hide you from us forever, that at the end the One who came will come back in power to work joy in us stronger even than death.   *Amen.*

Other Books by Seabury:

PERFECTED STEEL, TERRIBLE CRYSTAL: An Unconventional Source Book of Spiritual Readings in Poetry and Prose by Ned O'Gorman. A unique anthology of spiritual writing, including pieces by William Blake, Emily Dickenson, Dietrich Bonhoeffer and Pablo Neruda among others. A book for priests, students, thinkers and dreamers.
S-2330-X   pbk 272 pp.

TOWARD A NEW LIGHT by Carol Porter. A moving first novel of a woman's journey from the dark country of a scarred childhood to the light of faith and acceptance in maturity. A major selection of the *Christian Herald Family Bookshelf.*
S-0495-X   160 pp.

HOLINESS by Donald Nicholl
  "An excellent, succinct overview of Christian spirituality in its various forms . . . comprehensive, clear, finely balanced . . . highly recommended."—*Library Journal*
S-2336-9   168 pp.